MW00559743

GREAT LAKES SEA LAMPREY

GREAT LAKES SEA LAMPREY

THE 70 YEAR WAR ON A BIOLOGICAL INVADER

CORY BRANT

with a Foreword by Jerry Dennis

University of Michigan Press
Ann Arbor

Published in the United States of America by the
University of Michigan Press
Manufactured in the United States of America
Printed on acid-free paper
First published September 2019

A CIP catalog record for this book is available from the British Library.

Library of Congress Cataloging-in-Publication Data

Names: Brant, Cory, author.
Title: Great Lakes sea lamprey : the 70 year war on a biological invader / Cory Brant ;
    with a Foreword by Jerry Dennis.
Description: Ann Arbor : University of Michigan Press, 2019. | Includes
    bibliographical references and index.
Identifiers: LCCN 2019019137 (print) | LCCN 2019022303 (ebook) | ISBN
    9780472131563 (hardcover : alk. paper) | ISBN 9780472126033 (ebook)
Subjects: LCSH: Petromyzon marinus—Great Lakes (North America) | Biological
    invasions. | Introduced fishes.
Classification: LCC QL638.25.P48 B73   2019 (print) | LCC QL638.25.P48
    (ebook) | DDC 597/.2—dc23
LC record available at https://lccn.loc.gov/2019019137
LC ebook record available at https://lccn.loc.gov/2019022303

The University of Michigan Press gratefully acknowledges subventions from the Great
Lakes Fishery Commission in partial support of production costs for this volume.

Cover credit: Sea lamprey and lake trout. Photo by Andrea Miehls, GLFC and USGS
communications associate.

To sea lamprey control personnel, past, present, and future

FOREWORD

Jerry Dennis

When sea lamprey entered North America's Great Lakes in the 1930s, nobody could have anticipated the devastation they would unleash. Even now, in this era when we've become all too aware of the consequences of human meddling with ecosystems, it's difficult to imagine that a fishery as large and robust as the Great Lakes'—the most abundant freshwater fishery on the planet—could so quickly and utterly collapse.

Anyone who has spent time on or near the Great Lakes has probably witnessed firsthand the cascade of consequences set in motion by plants and animals that have been introduced intentionally or by accident. My own earliest memories are of looking across blue water extending to the horizon, then turning and seeing waist-high heaps of rotting and desiccated alewives as far as I could see up and down the beach. This was at the village of Empire, within view of Sleeping Bear Dunes, on what had previously been—and is, thankfully, now again—one of the finest sand beaches in the North American interior.

As this book so ably describes, the alewife was a six-inch-long fish from the Atlantic that entered the Great Lakes through the Erie and Welland Canals. It might never have had much impact if the sea lamprey, another fish native to the Atlantic, hadn't entered the lakes as well. The sea lamprey, a parasitic predator that feeds on larger fishes, found the lakes prime for conquest. Within a few years they had eliminated most of the lake trout, whitefish, and other predators that kept the alewife under control, allowing their population to explode. Some researchers estimate that by the 1960s alewives accounted for 80 percent of the biomass of all living things in the Great Lakes.

Cory Brant has done us a great favor in telling this story of cascading ecological events. He is a precise, thorough, and apparently tireless researcher with the writing chops to make the story fascinating, even to those of us without a background in the natural sciences. And the story *is* fascinating, and not only in the car-wreck-on-the-highway sense. If we were not so distracted by the sea lamprey's horror-movie appearance and gruesome habits we might more easily appreciate, as Dr. Brant does, that it is a "living fossil" with an interesting and highly unusual life history.

Other stories in the book are equally fascinating. The vivid account of the "pickle-jar" biology that led to the discovery of TFM, the selective lampricide that made it possible for the lakes to return to something like ecological balance, reads like a scientific detective story. Working seven days a week for years, a team of researchers performed tens of thousands of laboratory and field tests on more than 5,000 compounds in a search to find one that would kill larval sea lamprey in their natal rivers without harming other organisms. Success was in no way guaranteed, yet the researchers persisted despite dauntingly long odds, short budgets, and constant setbacks. It is because of their work that the Great Lakes can again support commercial and recreational fisheries.

But the story didn't end with the discovery of an effective lampricide. In fact, the story will never end. We can never let down our guard; sea lamprey and other invasive species are here to stay and require our constant vigilance and control. It is a cautionary tale for our times.

Perhaps the most important lesson to be learned is that efforts to control sea lamprey in the Great Lakes brought together previously isolated governments, agencies, and individuals into a model of cooperation that will benefit the lakes long into the future. In that sense, this history of an ecological disaster at least partially averted, is a story of hope.

CONTENTS

Preface | xi

Acknowledgments | xv

Introduction: A Biological Invader | 1

CHAPTER 1
An Ailing Ecosystem | 18

CHAPTER 2
The Deck of the *Beatrice M* | 42

CHAPTER 3
Nations Are Jolted to Action | 59

CHAPTER 4
First Stab at Sea Lamprey Control | 77

CHAPTER 5
Discovering a Chemical Assassin | 103

CHAPTER 6
Multinational AIS Control | 131

Conclusion | 144

Notes | 159

Index | 171

Illustrations following page 102

PREFACE

The fight against aquatic invasive species (AIS) is in the public eye more than ever. In recent years, national news outlets have run stories on "Asian carp," a term most commonly used in North America to refer to four separate species of fishes that were brought to the continent decades ago from China. Hundreds of millions of dollars have been invested to impede Asian carp, which are already entrenched throughout the Mississippi River and its tributaries. The objective is to stop these AIS from advancing into the Great Lakes via the Chicago River, with control efforts ranging from electric fences to "carpicides," high-frequency sounds, and carbon dioxide bubbles as deterrents. Of course, Asian carp are not the first invasive fishes to threaten the Great Lakes. For that matter, they're not even the first carp from Asia to invade the region—the common carp, native to lakes and rivers across Asia and Eastern Europe, was imported to North America in the nineteenth century and today remains widespread across the continental United States and Canada.[1] These invaders have even been found in Central and South America.[2] The common carp is particularly abundant throughout the Great Lakes Basin, and, though no sustainable control strategies currently exist for the species, scientists continue to study the fish's destructive impact on the ecosystem and to investigate new approaches to its management.[3]

This ongoing work by scientists, even in the face of what might appear to be a losing battle, is not unique to the case of the common carp. Even after public and media attention on a particular AIS fades, or shifts to the next new alien species threatening the Great Lakes, the work by scientists to manage earlier invaders usually carries on. A vivid example is the subject of this book, the fight against sea lampreys in the Great Lakes. By the late 1940s sea lampreys began to reach their peak destructive potential in the Great Lakes, which in turn sparked one of the earliest coordinated efforts to control an AIS in North America's history. While sea lampreys persist in the Great Lakes, and complete extirpation may never occur, scientists continue to improve techniques for monitoring and control.

My path studying sea lampreys began over a decade ago during my graduate work at Michigan State University. I focused on how and why sea lampreys use pheromones, and whether we can use these natural odors against them. I conducted my tests in the Ocqueoc River (a tributary of Lake Huron in Northern Michigan and a significant river in this story), and quickly realized I was studying sea lampreys in the same river where sea lamprey control began more than 70 years ago.

So many mysteries surround sea lampreys in the Great Lakes—I wanted to know the full story. How did sea lampreys get into the Great Lakes in the first place? How bad was the invasion? What lessons can be learned from the individuals that dealt with, or continue to deal with, invasive sea lampreys? Why are new Great Lakes researchers like me still searching for ways to control them?

In fall of 2015 I defended my dissertation and began a postdoctoral fellowship at the University of Michigan Water Center with a charge to answer these questions.

The sea lamprey story is captivating for many reasons, not least of all the nightmarish look of both the fish themselves and the damage they inflict on their prey. Perhaps what makes the sea lamprey story most intriguing, however, is that it's not just about the fight against a single AIS—it's the story of how modern fisheries management emerged in the Great Lakes. The sea lamprey invasion triggered an environmental awakening across the Great Lakes Basin, which includes all five Great Lakes (Superior, Michigan, Huron, Erie, and Ontario), their tributaries, and the land they drain into. In all, this is an area roughly the size of the United Kingdom, Spain, and Scotland combined. The Great Lakes are bordered by eight US states, the provinces of Ontario and Quebec, and multiple tribes and First Nations whose ancestors inhabited these shores long before Europeans arrived. The lamprey invasion dissolved political boundaries, sparked unprecedented cooperation, and led to an international treaty. A pioneering scientific spirit led to discoveries that are the backbone of a program that brought this creature under control and now protects the largest freshwater ecosystem in the world.

Too often we don't heed the lessons of those who witnessed mistakes in our past. While writing this book, I traveled the Great Lakes Basin to talk with individuals that still remember the worst of the sea lamprey invasion, those that were charged with developing the solution, and those that work in this program today. The hope is that, knowing their stories, we can better understand the future of sea lamprey control; how other, perhaps more insidious, invasive species have gone beneath our notice, and how we can better equip ourselves to stop those yet to come.

ACKNOWLEDGMENTS

Great Lakes Sea Lamprey has been one of the most rewarding research and writing experiences of my life. I have many to thank for helping to make this happen. First, I'd like to thank my advisors, Dr. Jennifer Read of the University of Michigan Water Center and Dr. Marc Gaden of the Great Lakes Fishery Commission, who together wrote the grant that funded this project. None of this would have happened without their collaboration and forward thinking. Special thanks to the University of Michigan Water Center, a center of the Graham Sustainability Institute, for supporting me with a postdoctoral fellowship during this research, and to the Great Lakes Fishery Commission for funding this research.

I thank Jerry Dennis, a truly inspiring outdoor writer, for taking time to write the foreword for this book. Scott Ham, acquiring editor with the University of Michigan Press, provided critical guidance throughout the writing process without losing his enthusiasm for sea lamprey history. Production editor Kevin Rennells and editorial associate Danielle Coty guided me through the production process. Elizabeth LaPorte, science outreach manager at the University of Michigan Graham Sustainability Institute, connected me with the U-M Press group and encouraged me every step of the way. I thank three anonymous peer reviewers for their expert guidance and comments. At the USGS Great Lakes Science Center, Tara Bell, technical information specialist, and Sofia Dabrowski, information services contractor, helped discover a wealth of resources at the John Van Oosten Library in Ann Arbor. Lauren Holbrook, communications associate at the Hammond Bay Biological Station, introduced me to Beatrice Skaggs and others with sea lamprey stories, assisted with interviews and permissions, and discovered, scanned, and preserved hundreds of photos and documents for the sea lamprey oral history project.

Many wonderful people met with me during research tours around the Great Lakes, helped with new contacts, assisted me in navigating countless backroads, and provided me with historical references. To them, I'm indebted: Stuart Sivertson, John Tibbles, Doug Garn, Ralph Wilcox, Dale Burkett, Jim McKane, Jean Adams, Lindsey Haskin, Shawn Nowicki, Mike Siefkes, Alex Gonzalez, Paul Sullivan, Gale Bravener, Pete Hrodey, Inger Schultz, Carol Brown, Jane Rumble, Megan Bresnahan, Roger Bergstedt, Randy Eshenroder, Jim Legualt, Tom Kuchenberg, Evelyn Sawyer, Charlie Haselrude, Sharalyn Johnston, Mylinda Woodward, Jennifer Despres, Rod MacDonald, Andrea Miehls, Dick Martin, Don Rutgers, Aaron Jubar, Don Loewen, Ellie Koon, and Christine Witulski. My U-M Undergraduate Research Opportunity Program student Jenna Rausch and research technician Ross Shaw helped me organize and edit hundreds of hours of transcripts from interviews, and I can't thank them enough.

Numerous organizations provided photographs, documents, or other references, or provided me a room to conduct interviews and dig through archival materials. I thank them all: US Fish and Wildlife Service, Chippewa Ottawa Resource Authority, Fisheries and Oceans Canada, Great Lakes Indian Fish and Wildlife Commission, New York State Department of Environmental Conservation, Michigan Department of Natural Resources, Wisconsin Department of Natural Resources, Ontario Ministry of Natural Resources and Forestry, Ontario Commercial Fisheries' Association, Ontario Federation of Anglers and Hunters, Superior Public Library, Alliance for the Great Lakes, NOAA Central Library, Bentley Historical Library, Dimond Library of the University of New Hampshire, Presque Isle County Historical Museum, Great Lakes Fishery Commission Archives, Sea Grant, Besser Museum for Northeast Michigan, Archives of Michigan, Tri-Cities Historical Museum, Archives of Ontario, Huronia Museum and Huron Ouendat Village, Leelanau Historical Society Museum, and the Great Lakes Fisheries Heritage Trail.

I'd like to credit B. G. Herbert Johnson, a pioneer sea lamprey control biologist with the Sea Lamprey Control Centre in Ontario, who wrote a detailed sea lamprey control history in the 1980s that was never published. His history was an invaluable reference while writing this book. I thank Devin Gill, stakeholder engagement specialist for the Cooperative Institute for Great Lakes Research, and the person that I'm fortunate to be married to, for her wisdom and encouragement, read-throughs of countless chapter drafts, and patience with her lamprey-obsessed husband. Lastly, I thank the many individuals whose stories are featured among these pages. They invited me to their homes and favorite coffee shops for interviews, allowed me to call and email them repeatedly with questions, and continue to help with the sea lamprey oral history project today.

In memory of Douglas "Doug" Cuddy (1946–2016),
Robert "Bob" Braem (1924–2017),
Clifford "Cliff" Kortman (1927–2017),
John Robertson (1942–2018),
Ralph Wilcox (1942–2019),
and Donald "Don" Allen (1937–2019).

Although we only spent a brief time together while writing this book, the fish stories, Great Lakes lessons, and laughs will not be forgotten.

INTRODUCTION

A Biological Invader

In the spring of 1949, Cliff Kortman wasn't sure what he was getting himself into as he headed down a sandy two-track toward a recently repurposed Civilian Conservation Corps (CCC) camp in northern Michigan. The camp was one of thousands peppered across the country—remnants of President Franklin D. Roosevelt's New Deal programs designed to provide the unemployed with work focusing on conservation and public infrastructure projects. This CCC camp rests near the shores of Lake Ocqueoc (pronounced "ah-kee-ock") in Millersburg, Michigan. The Ocqueoc River cuts through Ocqueoc Lake, state forest, and farmland and continues to meander several miles to where it spills into Lake Huron's Hammond Bay.

It wasn't a long trip to the camp for Cliff. He lived just on the other side of Ocqueoc Lake and grew up fishing and hunting with his family in the area. "We had a boat," the 87-year-old said in 2015 while sitting in his home in Rogers City, Michigan. "Oh, every night we would go down fishing."

Cliff knew something was wrong in Lake Huron. "We hardly had any fish at all in '49," he mentioned. The massive expanse of freshwater was in an ecological tailspin. Lake Michigan, Huron's hydrological twin, wasn't doing any better. Populations of slow-growing, native lake trout (*Salvelinus namaycush*) were crashing. Fishes of these freshwater seas had served as a supply of protein that fueled economic progress across North America for centuries. When the economy began to pick up following World War II, it placed increased commercial fishing pressure on the lakes. Yet within the Michigan waters of Lake Michigan annual lake trout catches went from 6.5 million pounds in 1944 to less than 400,000 by 1949.[1] By 1951 the total lake trout catch for all of Lake Michigan (Indiana, Wisconsin, Illinois, and Michigan combined) teetered at a mere

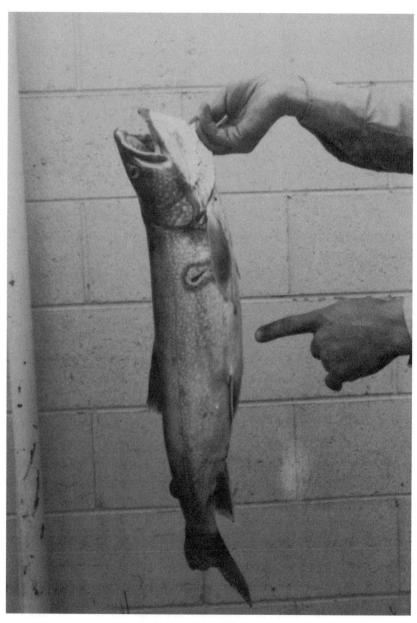

A lake trout caught in Lake Michigan showing strange wounds near Ludington, Michigan. (Photo courtesy of the Great Lakes Fishery Commission.)

11,000 pounds.[2] The complete eradication of lake trout was becoming a reality in Lake Michigan, and Lake Huron wasn't far behind. That fall of 1949 the Michigan Fish Commission (formed in 1873, the predecessor to today's Michigan Department of Natural Resources Fisheries Division) set more than 15,000 feet of net—nearly the length of 42 football fields—over a historically booming lake trout reef. The reef was off Waukegan, Illinois, in over 215 feet of water. They let their nets out for four days straight and caught only six peckish lake trout, five of which had strange rasping sores on their sides.[3]

Cliff's father once owned most of the land around the river on the other side of Ocqueoc Lake but was forced to sell about 18 acres of it during the Great Depression. Cliff farmed what was left during high school with his family but needed another source of income. When he pulled into the CCC camp, he met an ambitious University of Michigan graduate student named Vernon C. Applegate. Originally from New York City, Applegate had a Queens accent and an intense work ethic. He was based at the CCC camp, investigating a bizarre and destructive new creature that plagued the fishes in lakes Huron and Michigan. With just one more field season left to complete his PhD, he was quick to offer Cliff a job.

The work was unlike anything Cliff had ever known—a unique situation that would allow him to roll up his sleeves and work outdoors in a river he loved. He immediately took to the work alongside Applegate as a right-hand maintenance man and biological technician. Cliff didn't know it at the time, but he would spend the next 38 years of his life as one of the pioneer scientists that would turn the tide on the most destructive predator ever to enter the Laurentian Great Lakes. Cliff and Applegate were just a few of the hundreds who spent their careers combating this problem, a battle that continues today.

Nature of the Beast

So what *was* this biological invader that Cliff came face-to-face with in 1949? Anyone but Cliff might have turned and walked back out the door after Applegate revealed a specimen of the creature responsible for plaguing the fishery. It was a sea lamprey (*Petromyzon marinus*). In the Great Lakes, this animal garners about as much respect as a deer tick or a mosquito, yet it is far more sensational to lay eyes on.

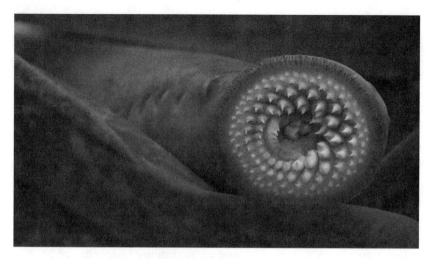

The sea lamprey up close. (Photo by the author.)

The sea lamprey is an outsider in the animal kingdom—it defies most of the basic traits seen across vertebrates. The organism is capable of traveling hundreds of miles upriver against swift currents with a snake-like swimming style. Its body is strong yet flexible, with cartilage rather than bones. Adult sea lampreys are sometimes mistakenly called "lamprey eels" or simply "eels" because of their body shape. These are not eels. Eels have jaws, bones, and paired fins (of the order Anguilliformes) while sea lampreys have no jaw, a cartilaginous skeleton, and no paired fins (order Petromyzontiformes).

The stealthy sea lamprey draws oxygen out of the water through a row of seven open gill pores on each side of its head. The barrel-shaped gills constantly contract and expand to push water like little hearts (unlike the C-shaped gills of a "typical" fish). The resemblance of the dark gill openings to the animal's eyes and nostrils even led early naturalists to mistakenly give sea lampreys the name *nine-eyes*, as on first glance the gills, eye, and nostril together give sea lamprey the appearance of having a row of nine eyes on each side of its head.[4]

This creature is one of the largest parasites on earth. It evolved an efficient way to feed long before animals could bite or chew. A jawless, suction-cup-like mouth containing rows of sharp teeth that look as though they've been stained with coffee adorns the sea lamprey's head.

Lake trout caught with a sea lamprey still attached, c. 1950s. (Photo courtesy of the John Van Oosten Library, US Geological Survey.)

Calling these "teeth" is incorrect; they're more like small horns made of keratin—a structural protein that also makes up our hair and fingernails. The animal vacuums itself to the side of an unsuspecting fish while the horn-teeth assist with grip. Thermal-sensitive cells inside the suction-cup mouth allow the parasite to distinguish between warm- and cold-blooded hosts. They're only interested in cold-blooded prey. Once firmly attached to a fish, a sharp beaklike tongue projects from the center of the sea lamprey's throat to wear away scales and break through capillaries. Specialized cells secrete an anticoagulant to keep blood flowing while hundreds of tiny fingerlike filaments around the mouth help maintain a tight seal on the victim. The unlucky host's health degrades as the parasite clings and feeds like a lazy hitchhiker. Sea lampreys will detach from a host if it dies and hunt down another. In just a little over a year, the sea lamprey consumes enough blood to grow from the length of a pinky finger to the length of a forearm. It's estimated that only one in seven fish attacked by a sea lamprey survives the experience.

A Fitting Host

Sea lampreys are choosy about their next meal when there are plenty of fish species to choose from. They prefer hosts that are large enough to stay alive during parasitism, are a reliable food source, and have scales that are easy to rasp away. The slow-growing, fatty lake trout, once mainstay of the Great Lakes fishery, makes a perfect target. No one knows exactly how a sea lamprey finds and attacks a host in an open lake or ocean. An attack has never been witnessed in the wild. In a laboratory tank, sea lampreys are often approached by a curious trout. A small parasitic sea lamprey looks a lot like a potential meal to larger fishes. As a trout closes in to bite, lampreys can quickly turn the tables and "bite" back, often attaching themselves near the gills or front fins of the trout. It's common to see scars near the gills or front-facing pectoral fins on wild-caught fishes that have survived lamprey attacks. Parasitic-phase lampreys have highly functioning eyes and a superior sense of smell coupled with a very stealthy swimming style. It's easy to picture one sneaking up on an unsuspecting host. Some fishes survive an attack and are left with varying levels of scarring, but most aren't so lucky. Severe scarring becomes increasingly rare to observe because those fishes are too weak to bite a fishing lure.

As lake trout and burbot (*Lota lota*), another native top predator in the Great Lakes, became less available, sea lampreys were quick to shift to the next available species. They weren't choosy at the peak of their Great Lakes invasion. They can attack and feed successfully on fishes ranging from a hand-sized yellow perch (*Perca flavescens*) to a human-sized lake sturgeon (*Acipenser fulvescens*), and they even somehow manage to catch the chrome rockets of the lakes, the Great Lakes rainbow trout (aka steelhead, *Oncorhynchus mykiss*).

Ancient Love Quest

The life history of a sea lamprey is as strange as its feeding habits. In the spring, full-grown parasites detach from their hosts out in the lake, cease to feed ever again, and begin their migratory phase. Adult sea lampreys move from deep water toward the shallows until they hit the shoreline. They continue to search the shallows until they encounter a river mouth, at which time they *may* decide to swim upstream. The river has to smell right to them; that is, it has to smell like young lampreys (larvae). Larval sea lampreys spend the first phase of their lives burrowed in the muddy bottoms of freshwater tributaries, and each "leaks" tiny amounts of a unique odor—it comes with their excrement. The cumulative smell of

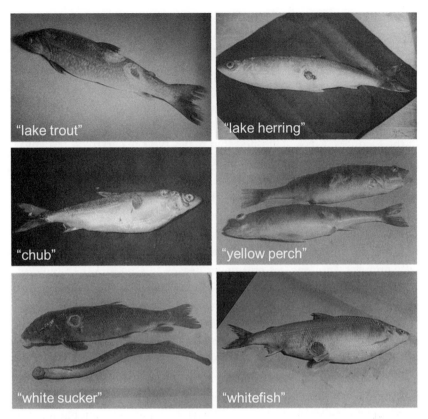

Various fish of the Great Lakes wounded by sea lampreys, c. 1940. Names in quotation marks were on backs of the photos. (Photos courtesy of the John Van Oosten Library, US Geological Survey.)

larvae creates a potent plume that travels down the length of the tributary to the river mouth. It's a chemical road map that only a sea lamprey can follow.[5] By following this chemical information, known as a conspecific cue, adult lampreys ensure that an energetically demanding migration will pay off. Adults that follow the larval odor plumes increase their likelihood of finding a suitable habitat in which their offspring can survive and thrive.[6]

The sea lamprey is nocturnal during its migration, which lasts from April to June. During this time, the lamprey's intestine, once thick and pink in color, turns into a tan, dead-looking strand of tissue not much wider than a guitar string. The liver turns as green as grass while hepatic ducts shut down and bile begins to accumulate in the failing organ. Death is on the horizon, but not before reproduction.

During the migratory phase, sea lampreys have been known to travel hundreds of miles up rivers to locate suitable spawning grounds—provided there isn't a dam or barrier to stop them. Prime sea lamprey spawning ground consists of areas with swift currents and gravel bottoms. Applegate, while studying thousands of migrating sea lampreys in the Ocqueoc River, suggested that males typically arrive at spawning grounds early to begin the incredible task of nest building. The suction-cup mouth, once used to parasitize fishes, is now a tool used to rearrange the stream bed for nesting. Both male and female sea lampreys use their mouths to move rocks in the stream and create a nest. When Carl Linnaeus gave the sea lamprey its scientific name in the mid-1700s, he chose *Petromyzon marinus* (stone, to suckle; pertaining to the sea).

Centuries later the act still never ceases to amaze. When building its nest, a large sea lamprey can move stream rocks up to the size of softballs, though most are golf-ball-sized or smaller. It's an impressive feat for an organism with no arms, legs, or even paired fins. Finer sediments are cleared with violent tail fans. Larger rocks are piled at the downstream end of the nest until a U-shaped dugout, sometimes as big as a garbage can lid, takes shape in the stream bed. The old phrase "work smarter, not harder" applies to lampreys as well: they will sometimes take over an old trout spawning bed where half of the work has already been done. The male feels around the nest with his mouth to a seemingly fussy extent. Males are territorial—a fight usually breaks out if another male intrudes. The nesting male grabs and shakes the intruder as they tumble downstream like a couple of drunks in a bar brawl. The winner usually meanders back up to the nest, and the loser moves on to find his own nesting spot.

Love is all about chemistry, and that's especially true in sea lampreys. Nesting is where the sea lamprey's second form of chemical communication comes into play. Once a male has established a nest and is ready to mate, an odorless and colorless *love cocktail* begins to leak from the gills. It's a sex pheromone, mainly made up of bile alcohols, some of which are the same compounds released by larvae with their waste. The pheromone is ignored by other species, yet female sea lampreys can smell it for miles downstream. This pheromone signal, if we could see it, would be similar to rolling a red carpet down the river leading directly

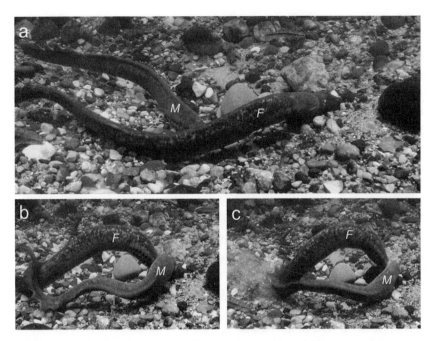

Spawning sea lampreys in the Trout River near Rogers City, Michigan, June 11, 2013. (a), a male approaching a female in a nest; (b), the male attaching itself to the female's head with coiled tails; (c) the spawning vibration. (Photos by the author.)

to the mate-ready male. Females, with one-third of their brains devoted to olfaction, follow the pheromone plume with pinpoint accuracy. It's another ancient adaptation assuring that potential mates will meet.[7]

Once a female enters the nest things heat up. Males develop a distinctive ridge of tissue along the length of their backs, a conspicuous secondary sexual characteristic nicknamed "the rope," as they mature. The rope is comprised of fat loaded with energy-producing cells known as mitochondria, similar to brown fat in young mammals, and heats up a few tenths of a degree in the presence of females.[8] Thermally sensitive cells in a lamprey's mouth can detect tiny changes in temperature, and both males and females repeatedly "feel" each other with their mouths in the nest. All this has led scientists to hypothesize that heat plays a role in sea lamprey courtship.

The act of mating in sea lampreys is unique. Females will attach to a larger structure at the top of the nest such as a large rock or log; even a mud-filled beer bottle works pretty well. After a great deal of back-and-forth touching, the male runs along the back of a female and attaches himself to the back of her head. They immediately coil tails. The male flexes into a U-shape, which bends the female's body into the same position. The two engage in an intense vibration that creates a cloud of sediment, eggs, and sperm in the water. Fertilization occurs on the rocks, which at this point have been strategically placed at the downstream end of the nest.

After spawning, adult sea lampreys are rotten parents. The parents are literally dead and rotten by the time larvae hatch, and it's a natural part of their life history. Because sea lampreys invest all their energy in a single reproductive season, their reproductive output is incredibly high. Females are effectively a swimming tube of eggs at the peak of the spawning season. Each female typically produces around 150,000 eggs, yet up to 250,000 have been counted.[9] If only 3% of these eggs actually develop into larvae, an estimate on the safe side according to scientists,[10] one female can still produce 5,000 offspring. A single sea lamprey can consume up to 30% of its own body weight in blood per day, translating to roughly 40 pounds of fish, during its 18-month parasitic phase.[11] That means the combined offspring from one female could theoretically kill over 100,000 pounds of fish in the Great Lakes.

The sperm and eggs of sea lampreys continue to captivate scientists. Once released into the water, eggs develop sticky bottoms, which allow them to adhere to rocks in just the right position to help the sperm hit at the terminal end of the egg. Sea lampreys' sperm are hypothesized to have the ability to "smell" the eggs. Laboratory studies suggest that spermatozoa become more active when exposed to water that had previously contained eggs.[12] Taking a closer look, a recent study suggests that the sperm have chemoreceptors, special odor-detection neurons similar to those found in adult lamprey for detecting pheromones, which scientists believe help sperm locate eggs. The next step for scientists is to test this theory by placing the sperm in a small maze to see if they consistently swim toward a source of eggs.[13]

After a little over a week of incubation, the newly hatched larval sea lampreys are no bigger than an eyelash. They stay among the rocks for another week. It's during this time that they develop some pigmentation and a specialized mouth called a buccal hood. Blind and clumsy, they drift downstream until they hit stream sediment where they can bur-

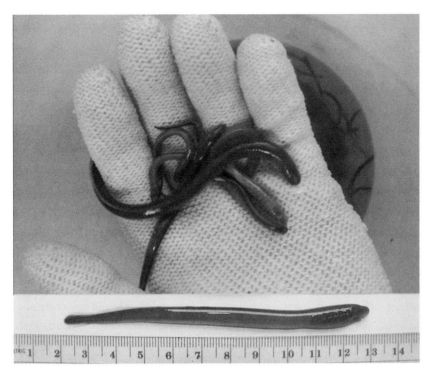

Larval sea lampreys collected by the author from a stream in Tawas, Michigan, in 2013. (Photos by the author.)

Larval sea lampreys collected by the author while electrofishing. (Photos by the author.)

row. Larvae prefer sand or silt sediment. They often position themselves along or near the main current, usually around spots with some aquatic weeds mixed in. They're reclusive filter feeders at this stage, poking their hood-shaped mouths out of their burrows at night to catch food particles in the current.

Growing into the Perfect Parasite

For centuries it was believed that larval sea lampreys, once called "mud eels," were an entirely different organism from adults. The mistake is reasonable, as they look nothing like their adult form. At the larval stage, eyes are no more than darkened pigment spots. The gills resemble a single notchy slash along each side of the head that look like fresh scars from stitches. When larval sea lampreys are released into an aquarium with sand at the bottom, they immediately swim down. They continue to swim until they bury their faces in the sand. Once halfway burrowed, their bodies stop moving, and they seem to mysteriously sink the rest of the way into the sediment with no visible movement. What they are actually doing is repeatedly pointing and expanding their mouths, like the foot of a clam, to "walk" their faces deeper into the sediment without moving their bodies.[14] It's mesmerizing. The larvae turn upward in their burrows until their heads can just barely pop back out of the sand. The U-shaped burrow allows water to flow through and irrigate their gills while they remain positioned, ready to poke their heads out just far enough to safely feed on plankton and other plant particles.

In the 1960s, Applegate made an important discovery that would eventually be a game changer in the fight against Great Lakes sea lampreys. He discovered that while sea lampreys typically remain in the larval stage in streams for 4 to 5 years, under some conditions they can remain larval for up to 17 years. Then, for reasons still relatively unknown to science, something triggers the larvae to begin the transformation into the adult stage by the thousands. On land this event would be comparable to a cicada hatch, which also occurs when massive numbers of dirt-dwelling larvae transform into adults after 2 to 17 years of hiding. However, unlike cicadas, which fly into the trees to sing the mating songs that remind us of summer, sea lampreys in the Great Lakes transform into lethal predators that move downstream in search of prey.

A larval lamprey's body is physiologically rearranged during its transformation into the parasitic phase. The transformation can take months,

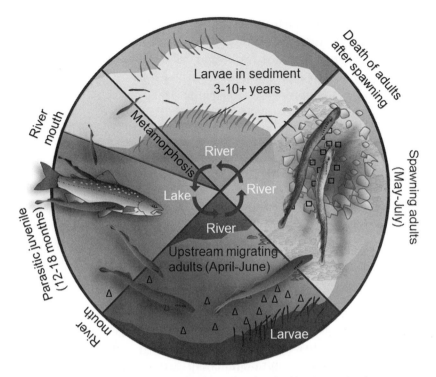

Life cycle of the sea lamprey, drawn by the author, inspired by Vernon Applegate and Cliff Kortman's early work. Triangles indicate a pheromone released by larvae in streams, which functions as a migratory cue. Squares indicate a mating pheromone released by males, which helps draw females into a nest for courtship.

over which time the harmless, filter-feeding, "buccal hood" mouth turns into a toothy suction cup. Highly functioning eyes develop from gray spots, while the gills are completely renovated. Two distinctive dorsal fins become visible along its back, allowing for efficient, snakelike swimming. Newly transformed sea lampreys move downstream to the lake, typically in masses during midwinter, and begin their parasitic phase. The parasitic adults feed on fishes for about 18 months. When they head to a river to spawn, the life cycle is complete.

Parasite Turns Predator

The sea lamprey is native to the sea—its range includes the Atlantic Ocean and tributaries throughout the eastern US and western European coasts. So how can a primarily marine dwelling species such as the lamprey even survive in the freshwater Great Lakes? Similar to salmon, sea lampreys are anadromous, meaning they've evolved to live in marine water and then move into freshwater tributaries to spawn. They've always been able to adjust to freshwater life, at least temporarily. Also like salmon, sea lampreys are semelparous; they invest all their energy in a single reproductive season and die shortly afterward. This life cycle helps ensure that sea lampreys will have an ecologically stable place in their native range. Out in the ocean, adult sea lampreys prey on much larger fishes such as tuna and grouper; they have even been known to hitch rides on basking sharks and feed on the cold skin of marine mammals like minke whales.[15] These marine species evolved alongside the lampreys and can survive the parasitic encounter, often left with not much more than an unsightly scar. By the time sea lampreys in their native range enter freshwater for spawning, the parasitic stage of life has already ended, meaning that smaller, freshwater fishes are not at risk of attack.

North America has a love/hate relationship with sea lampreys because of their destructive nature in a nonnative range and their threatened status in a native range. Where they occur naturally, sea lampreys actually serve several important functions. Striped bass (*Morone saxatilis*) and swordfish (*Xiphias gladius*) have been reported to eat marine sea lampreys.[16] Birds and small mammals capitalize on an easy meal when sea lampreys are spawning by the thousands in shallow freshwater tributaries. The bodies of sea lampreys that die after spawning fertilize tributaries in their native range, creating a link through which nutrients can move from the sea into freshwater environments.[17]

Sea lampreys aren't native to the Great Lakes, but this doesn't mean the lakes were lamprey-free before sea lampreys arrived. Four native lamprey species were already there. Native Great Lakes lamprey species include silver lampreys (*Ichthyomyzon unicuspis*) and chestnut lampreys (*Ichthyomyzon castaneus*), both of which evolved to grow to a much smaller adult size to match with smaller native fishes. Two additional native lamprey species in the Great Lakes Basin, the northern brook lamprey (*Ichthyomyzon fossor*) and the American brook lamprey (*Lethenteron appendix*), don't parasitize fishes at all—they eat algae and plankton and never leave the rivers. These four native lamprey species are misunderstood and vital members of a healthy ecosystem.

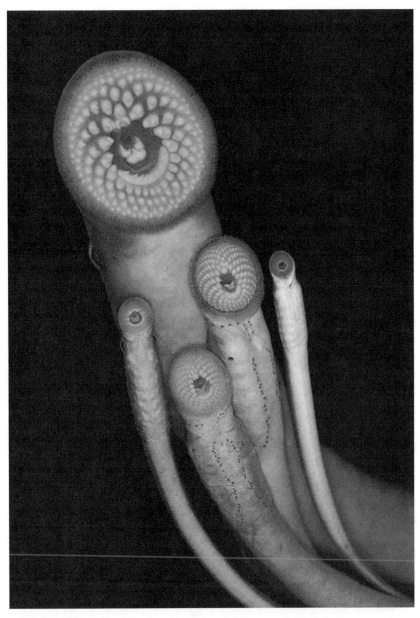

There are five lamprey species in the Great Lakes, four native and one invasive. An invasive sea lamprey (*top*) is pictured along with the four native lamprey species: (*left to right*) American brook lamprey, chestnut lamprey, silver lamprey, and northern brook lamprey. (Photo by Andrea Miehls, Great Lakes Fishery Commission and US Geological Survey.)

Model Organisms

Sea lampreys, as organisms, are remarkable. Lampreys are living fossils. They've remained mostly unchanged for more than 300 million years.[18] Lampreys existed on Earth for 150 million years before the evolution of dinosaurs, whose reign on the planet ended more than 65 million years ago. According to the fossil record, lampreys persisted through the ages—surviving at least four mass extinctions. Consider them the cockroaches of the aquatic world. Today there are 39 species of lampreys inhabiting environments ranging from the frozen Arctic and Pacific drainages of Alaska to the wave-pounded river mouths that empty into the Tasman Sea off the coast of New Zealand.[19] Lampreys were here long before humans, and they'll be here long after we're gone.

Given how ancient lampreys are, they can be seen as a kind of "living template" for the origin of vertebrates. The scientific discoveries with sea lampreys have been extensive—partly because a huge supply of research specimens is removed from the Great Lakes by sea lamprey control crews each year. Sea lampreys are model organisms around the world for studies in vertebrate evolution, ecology, developmental biology, medicine, chemistry, and much more.

Researchers at Michigan State University recently began studying an incredible phenomenon in larval sea lampreys in hopes of improving human medicine. During their transformation from larvae to juvenile parasite, a sea lamprey naturally undergoes a shutdown of bile ducts in the liver—a condition in infant humans known as biliary atresia, which causes fibrosis and requires a liver transplant. By the time a sea lamprey is fully parasitic, all of the signs of biliary atresia are gone and the liver turns from green to pink.[20] It's likely that sea lampreys offer a mechanism for possible therapy for infant biliary atresia.[21] A Google Scholar search for "sea lamprey, evolution," will get you more than 23,000 hits in less than 0.07 seconds. Sea lamprey pheromone research has led to more than 2,000 studies since 1995—studies that have helped us understand how animals, including humans, communicate.

The fascinating scientific side of sea lampreys is often overshadowed by the sensational look of the organism itself. As you can imagine, sea lampreys have been the inspiration for a handful of low-budget horror movies along with countless magazine articles and books. They've been referred to as bloodthirsty predators, vampires of the deep, and even a

Sensational media images like these weren't uncommon at the peak of the sea lamprey's destruction in the Great Lakes, even though sea lampreys don't attack people. (Photo by the author.)

Great Lakes' Dracula. Nothing will make you do the "get-off-me dance" quite like a sea lamprey firmly attached to your hand. The March 10, 1965, issue of the *Toledo Blade* quoted attorney General Nicholas Katzenbach describing organized crime in the United States as "a nationwide conspiracy which is attached, like a lamprey eel, to the body of our society" involving billions of dollars and accounting for scores of murders and untold horrors.[22] The intimidating look of the lamprey coupled with the damage it deals was the inspiration for the World War II submarine *USS Lamprey* (*SS-372*), a Balao class sub with a long line of open ports along each side of the hull. The Manitowoc Shipbuilding Company completed and launched the sub June 1944 for testing in Lake Michigan.

CHAPTER 1

AN AILING ECOSYSTEM

When Cliff Kortman began working with Vernon Applegate in Northern Michigan there were only a handful of invasive species in the Great Lakes. Common carp and a few other smaller nonnative fishes with normal-looking fins and mouths had been around since the 1920s. Nothing like a sea lamprey had ever shown up. Since then more than 100 nonnative species have appeared. We are only beginning to understand the ecological and economic impacts resulting from a constant titration of new organisms into the Great Lakes.

In the case of sea lampreys, everyone could tell they were destructive just by looking at them. The *Mr. Hyde* side of most new organisms isn't always as clear. This begs the question: what makes a newcomer "invasive"?

Tasty Invaders

To answer that question, it's helpful to look back to events that occurred decades before Cliff's introduction to the sea lamprey. On April 4, 1912, workers from the Michigan Fish Commission hauled box upon box of tiny, fertilized, milky-colored eggs to the shore of 19-mile-long Torch Lake, an inland lake near Traverse City, Michigan. Torch is less than a mile from Grand Traverse Bay in Lake Michigan. Each box was loaded into boats and dumped into Torch's clear blue waters—roughly 6 million eggs. A few days later, on April 6, the rest of the shipment, 16 million eggs, were dumped into Crystal Lake just a few miles west of Traverse City.[1] These weren't lamprey eggs.

The two lakes were receiving a payload of viable rainbow smelt (*Osmerus mordax*) eggs. A slender, silvery fish that grows to about nine inches long, rainbow smelt are another anadromous Atlantic Ocean species with the same native range as sea lampreys. These eggs came from a freshwater population in Green Lake, Maine. Smelt are adaptable to freshwater too. As it was a popular fish on the East Coast, the idea was to bring the species west for food and recreation. A stream connects Crystal Lake to the Betsie River, which in turn flows into Lake Michigan near Frankfort. The smelt thrived as they spread across the two lakes. About a decade later, massive glittering schools of rainbow smelt began appearing in Lake Michigan. Unlike the sea lampreys, smelt were met with open arms—or, rather, nets.

"Coho fever" is commonly referred to as the first fishing frenzy to sweep across the Great Lakes. Hard-fighting Pacific coho salmon were stocked in Lake Michigan in the mid-1960s, and the species quickly became a key target for recreational and charter fishers. But those that lived around the basin in the '40s and '50s would argue that "smelt fever" came first and was even bigger. Lake trout were already beginning to decline by the end of the 1930s due to overfishing, pollution, and habitat loss, and sea lampreys were beginning the process of finishing them off. This allowed smelt to spread unchecked by natural predators throughout Lake Michigan. Populations of the tasty little fish exploded. Smelt netting parties during the spring smelt run became traditions along the streams and river mouths. In the winter, entire communities would form on frozen bays. A commercial market sprang up across the basin as smelt expanded their new range. Lake Michigan's annual commercial harvest of smelt reached 9 million pounds by 1958. The harvest in the US and Ontario waters of Lake Erie was twice as productive at just over 19 million pounds annually by 1962.[2] In short, despite the fact that it was a nonnative species, smelt weren't seen as a threat to the Great Lakes. They mostly still aren't. Yet there's an ecological dark side to smelt perhaps as dark as the sea lamprey.

Dr. Howard Tanner is the former Michigan Department of Natural Resources (DNR) director who made the decision, with Dr. Wayne Tody (also formerly of the department's Fisheries Division), to introduce Pacific salmon into the Great Lakes in the 1960s. The story of stocking salmon in the Great Lakes is a big one, as the decision created a world-class Pacific salmon fishery 2,000 miles inland from the Pacific coast, but it's not the main reason I traveled to Howard's home in south-central Michigan in 2016. Howard remembers the hype that erupted in Michigan around smelt. "We talk about sea lamprey, but as a teenager I

Smelt-dipping madness in Cold Creek, a tributary of Crystal Lake near Beulah, Michigan, c. 1930s. (Real photo postcard, courtesy of the Great Lakes Fishery Commission.)

experienced the smelt runs," the 92-year-old said with a grin. "The winter smelt fishing on Lake Charlevoix—Smeltania they called it." Howard explained that it was a winter festival to celebrate the smelt. There were smelt wrestling matches and, yes, even a smelt queen. Smeltanias popped up all over the lakes as far north as Escanaba, Michigan. "They ran electricity and telephone wires out to the shanties. It was a village out there. Everybody was catching smelt," Howard said.

Howard never considered the destructive potential of smelt as a kid, but his views changed after a lifelong career with the Great Lakes fishery. "There were a lot of smelt, and smelt are a predator—in the same time zone, same habitat, as the lake trout," Howard said as we chatted about smelt teeth. "When those little lake trout came out of the gravel, I think the smelt were an overlooked added burden on the viability of the lake trout population." Smelt were eating young lake trout before the trout had a chance to grow up and eat smelt.

Retired commercial fishers across the Great Lakes Basin agree—smelt were destructive during their peak infestation. Smelt may even have been destructive as a food source for trout. Jim MacDonald, a longtime commercial fisherman from Sault Ste. Marie, Ontario, remembers lake trout caught in Lake Huron near Tobermory, Ontario, in the 1960s

Dipping smelt from a pound net through the ice in Lake Michigan's Little Bay de Noc, near Escanaba, Michigan, on March 4, 1941. (Photo courtesy of the John Van Oosten Library, US Geological Survey.)

not looking so good after eating primarily smelt. He mentioned that it was clear from cleaning the lake trout that the stomachs had been punctured by partially digested jawbones. Lake trout that had been eating smelt seemed less healthy, with a greenish bilelike liquid accumulated around the guts. Smelt jaws would "fowl up" Jim's nets and cut his hands. "You had hundreds of those jawbones to every nine feet of cork," he said, as we chatted about his old fishing days in Sault Ste. Marie. It was a side to smelt that no one except commercial fishers would have seen.

Traveling along the southwest shore of Lake Superior, I tracked down Mark Rude—a retired multigenerational commercial fisherman whose family once had a fishing base on Isle Royale in Lake Superior. The 45-mile-long island and its surrounding 450 smaller islands were Mark's summer home as a kid. He remembers the mid-twentieth-century smelt frenzies that erupted near Superior, Wisconsin. "By the early '50s, people were going down to Park Point along the river mouths and just taking dip nets and filling 50 gallon drums with smelt. I don't know what the heck they did with them," he laughed. "I think they probably fertilized a lot of rosebushes down in Minneapolis." We sat and drank black coffee

A cooler full of smelt caught in Lake Michigan by the author in 2013. (Photo by the author.)

in his home near Duluth, Minnesota, all evening and talked about smelt, sea lampreys, and commercial fishing near Isle Royale.

Mark mentioned that at one point in the 1960s he and his crew hoisted what he estimates as more than 10,000 pounds of smelt, slightly heavier than a full-grown hippo, from Lake Superior near Duluth. This was a single net lift.

Invasive or Introduced?

Sea lampreys and smelt are not native in the Great Lakes, yet the former is often referred to as an invasive species while the latter is labeled an introduced species. This creates blurry lines for definitions related to newcomer organisms.

There are many terms used to describe a species that doesn't belong in a certain ecosystem—*non-indigenous species, non-native species, nuisance species, invasive species,* and *alien species* are a few. Perhaps it's best to stay with legal definitions. According to the US Department of Agriculture's Executive Order 13751, titled "Safeguarding the Nation from the Impacts of Invasive Species," signed by President Barack Obama on December 5, 2016 (an amendment to EO 13112, "National Invasive Species Council," signed by President Bill Clinton on February 8, 1999), an *invasive species* is "an alien species whose introduction does or is likely to cause economic or environmental harm or harm to human health." An *alien species* is "any species, including its seeds, eggs, spores, or other biological material capable of propagating that species, that is not native to that ecosystem." *Introduction* is defined as "the intentional or unintentional escape, release, dissemination, or placement of a species into an ecosystem as a result of human activity." In other words, all invasive species are alien species, but not all alien species are considered invasive (i.e., the introduced Pacific salmon and rainbow trout of the Great Lakes are not considered invasive).

Similar language is used across the border in Canada. According to the province's Invading Species Awareness Program, established in 1992 by the Ontario Federation of Anglers and Hunters (OFAH) in partnership with the Ontario Ministry of Natural Resources and Forestry, *alien species* are "species of plants, animals (including fish), and micro-organisms introduced by human action outside of their natural past of present distribution." Similarly, *invasive alien species* are "those harmful alien species whose introduction or spread threatens the environment, the economy, or society, including human health." For simplicity's sake, I'll continue to refer to aquatic invasive species as AIS in the rest of this story.

The US Fish and Wildlife Service (USFWS) Stop Aquatic Hitchhikers Program and Ontario's Invading Species Awareness Program—provides many resources educators, lake associations, and anglers can use to help stop the introductions and spread of AIS.[3]

An AIS Injection

Smelt and common carp are some of the earliest introduced species in the Great Lakes. Both of these cases are examples of introductions that were conducted on purpose, under the assumption that having these creatures in our waters would somehow boost the economy. But today AIS are entering the Great Lakes through many human-related vectors, whether we know it or not. New creatures enter the Great Lakes via our

In this photo, taken in 1990, zebra mussels encrust a native Unionid mussel. The bottom half of the native mussel was under the sediment. (Photo 1990-C-2, courtesy of the John Van Oosten Library, US Geological Survey.)

shipping industries or channel construction; via recreational activities like water sports, fishing, and hunting; and through intentional introductions, as pet releases, and much more. The damage that an AIS can inflict on an ecosystem is not always as conspicuous as the rasping holes sea lampreys inflict on fishes. This creates a problem for the Great Lakes. If the damage is out of sight, it's out of mind. Just underneath the surface, the scene could be as jolting as a decaying carpet of invasive mussels. Anyone who enjoys walking along Great Lakes shorelines will only notice the rolling waves.

Zebra and quagga mussels, two separate species commonly called dreissenid mussels, were not met with an international uproar upon their arrival in the Great Lakes. Zebras (*Dreissena polymorpha*) first appeared in Lake St. Clair in 1986. Quaggas (*Dreissena rostriformis bugensis*) showed up a few years later, in 1989, in Lake Erie.[4] Both mussels are native to a region between Europe and Asia. Both species have a free-swimming, microscopic planktonlike stage and a sedentary stage attach to the bottom of the lakes. Both made their way into the Great Lakes via the bellies of ships—in the ballast water of international freighters. Both have completely changed the ecosystem of the Great Lakes forever.

How did freighters that had been floating in waters of the former Soviet Union wind up near Detroit with bellies full of invasive species? In the mid-1980s, US farmers were hit with the worst economic crisis since the Great Depression, the epicenter of which was the Midwest. Like most economic crises, this one began in the best of times. Following World War II, a boom in agricultural technology, pesticide production, and fertilizers led to a significant US food surplus by the 1960s. Stockpiles of food dwindled by the 1970s while at the same time global demand for US agricultural products was snowballing.

In 1972 the Soviet Union experienced below-average agricultural production and negotiated a contract with the United States to purchase agricultural products.[5] A few years later, in 1979, the Carter administration enacted a grain embargo against the Soviet Union in response to the Soviets' invasion of Afghanistan. The embargo was lifted by the Reagan administration in 1981—helping the Republican president win support in the Midwest. A side effect was fleets of rusting freighters originating in the dreissenid mussels' native range making regular trips to Midwest ports via Great Lakes shipping routes.

Many of these ships arrived with ballast tanks containing millions of gallons of water from their home ports, giving the otherwise empty vessels additional weight to help with stability on the ocean voyage. After loading new freight in the United States, this additional weight was no longer needed, and the ships would purge their ballast water—and any hitchhikers living in it—before embarking for home. It was a direct injection of Caspian and Black Sea waters into the Great Lakes.

Invasive species can outcompete other invasive species, and that isn't a good thing. Nearly 30 years after the two dreissenid mussels were introduced into the Great Lakes, the more broadly adaptive quagga mussel reigns supreme. Zebra mussels are adapted to living in slightly warmer water and attaching to relatively hard substrates like native mussel shells, rocks, piers, and boat hulls. Quagga mussels are adapted to living in a broader range of temperatures, can tolerate colder water temperatures than zebras, and can live on softer substrates, allowing them to establish themselves in deeper waters and more diverse environments compared

The ocean-going freighter *Federal Maas* cruises the St. Clair River in 2012. (Photo courtesy of Marc Gaden, Great Lakes Fishery Commission.)

to their cousins. Zebra mussels are actually becoming rarer in the Great Lakes, but they are continuing to sweep west across North America.

In a scientific cry for action, researchers from all over North America immediately warned that the dreissenid invasion needed to be taken seriously. From 1988 to 1998 more than 350 peer-reviewed studies were published related to the outbreak on such subjects as natural history, ecological impacts, ballast management, and control. While researchers' warnings were generally ignored, Capitol Hill perked up when the invasive mussels fowled municipal water intake pumps near Monroe, Michigan, causing citywide water outages.

Public outcry prompted Congress to enact the Nonindigenous Aquatic Nuisance Prevention and Control Act of 1990 (NANPCA), a measure that aimed to deal with untreated ballast water, develop control and removal methods for newcomers such as dreissenids, and prevent new invasions. But action came slowly, and the NANPCA went cold while both of these invasive mussels remain unchecked in their new home and continue to sweep their way across North America. As the new mussels spread, so did the public outcry to take action against them. Dreissenid mussels clogged water intake pipes,[6] encrusting docks and boats, and cut the hands and feet of people trying to enjoy Great Lakes beaches.

Six years later the original act was expanded into the National Invasive Species Act (NISA). It updated NANPCA by "encouraging" all ships entering US waters to exchange their ballast water outside the 200-mile US Exclusive Economic Zone and by requesting that these ships report whether or not they had actually done so. The geographic scope of the act was also expanded to include areas outside the Great Lakes region. While NISA continues to take action against invasive species, it's still not clear who has the authority to sterilize the ballast water of ships that regularly travel across boundaries. New creatures are still being injected directly into the heart of the Great Lakes.

The influx of species into the Great Lakes via shipping ballast has slowed since the St. Lawrence Seaway Management Corporation, formerly known as the St. Lawrence Seaway Authority, an organization established in 1998 by the Canadian government, made it mandatory that all transoceanic ships entering the Great Lakes exchange their ballast tanks. Ships bound for Canadian ports were required to do so in 2006, and ships bound for US ports were required to do so in 2008. Since then only two new species—bloody-red shrimp (*Hemimysis anomala*) in 2006 and a zooplankton (*Thermocyclops crassus*) in 2014—have been reported.[7] Most agree that flushing ballast water helps, but it doesn't stop everything.

Tom Nalepa, a 35-year veteran of the National Oceanic and Atmospheric Administration's (NOAA) Great Lakes Environmental Research Laboratory (GLERL) in Ann Arbor, Michigan, conducted foundational work on invasive dreissenid mussels in the Great Lakes. Since the 1980s, Tom had worked with a team that regularly sampled sediments around the southern basin of the Great Lakes. The mission was to look for changes that had been occurring around the lake bottom since the 1960s. "We sampled in 1986–87 and again in 1992–93—just a few years after zebra mussels had gotten in," Tom told me as we chatted at the university's Water Center.

In the fall of 1992, Tom made a menacing discovery that helped us begin to understand the irreversible damage these thumbnail-sized invaders can cause. Tom discovered that a tiny shrimplike organism that lives in bottom sediments, scientifically known as Diporeia, disappears once dreissenid mussels become abundant. In the late 1980s, if you were to examine an area of the lake bottom one meter square virtually anywhere in the deeper areas of the Great Lakes, there would have been

10,000 to 20,000 of these rice-sized relatives of krill scurrying around in the upper layers of sediment. "Usually Diporeia are scrambling all over in the sample when it gets up to the boat," Tom explained. "That fall of 1992, while sampling the same locations, we found none."

Diporeia are nutrient and calorie rich. Around 30% to 40% of their bodies are made up of healthy fats and oils. For thousands of years they were the main food source of lake whitefish (*Coregonus clupeaformis*), and the two species create a link that allows energy to flow from the lake bottom to the top of the food web. Tom mentioned that to this day no one can fully explain why Diporeia populations decline to zero in the presence of dreissenids. Research suggests it may be due to a combination of factors, including a decrease in the quantity and quality of food resulting from the filtering activities of the mussels and increased susceptibility to diseases and pathogens.[8] "There isn't a single process in the Great Lakes, physical, chemical, or biological, that hasn't been affected directly or indirectly by dreissenid mussels," Tom added.

Dreissenid mussels carpet the lake bottoms with dense colonies and can be found on all types of substrate, both hard (rock, gravel) and soft (mud). Like sea lampreys, one female dreissenid mussel can produce several hundred thousand eggs. Dreissenids attach to the shells of native mussels and basically smother them. Native mussels are now extirpated from the open waters of the Great Lakes. Dense dreissenid colonies act like giant water filters. By filtering out all the food particles, energy becomes increasingly tied up at the lake bottom, in invasive mussel biomass or deposited feces, leaving little food to support small native organisms in the rest of the water column that historically served as food for Great Lakes fishes.

Diporeia are disappearing, whitefish populations are unstable, and the water column is becoming increasingly clear. A single dreissenid mussel filters two liters of water a day. The clearing water allows light to penetrate deeper into the historically dark reaches of the lakes. Increasing light penetration allows algae such as *Cladophora* (sometimes called "angel hair" because of its flowing underwater appearance) to expand its range and grow thick. As rotting algae and alien mussels continue to accumulate, it promotes the growth of the bacterium *Clostridium botulinum*. The name is immediately familiar to people. This bacterium produces the type E botulism toxin, and the toxin concentrates in and around the mussels. The unpredictable nature of AIS gets worse.

A round goby rests on invasive dreissenid mussels. (Photo by Eric Engbretson, US Fish and Wildlife Service, via Wikimedia Commons.)

Round Goby

Like clockwork, another introduction occurred via international shipping ballast water around the same time as dreissenid mussels. The round goby (*Neogobius melanostomus*), a small yet high-strung bottom-dwelling fish historically native to the same region as the dreissenid mussels, reared its bug-eyed head in the St. Clair River in 1990. These gobies, which had adapted to eat dreissenid mussels back home, began eating toxic ones in the Great Lakes. Gobies accumulate toxins in their guts, and can become partially paralyzed due to the specific neurotoxin released by *C. botulinum*.

A leading hypothesis among researchers suggests that partially paralyzed gobies, and perhaps other fishes that ate them, were then eaten by various water birds. To everyone's horror, birds began to fall from the skies in the early 2000s. An estimated 50,000 birds around the Great

Lakes died of botulism poisoning in just four years.[9] Now, round gobies outcompete all other smaller fishes for food and habitat along the rocky shallows across most of the Great Lakes.

Some may wonder why we don't let new species continue to enter and mix with native species until things balance out. It has also been suggested that we focus our prevention efforts on those species *known* to be harmful while giving new species deemed *safe* a free pass. Looking back at sea lampreys, smelt, round gobies, common carp, and dreissenid mussels, it's clear that we can't always predict which AISs will be harmful and which won't. How do we, an organism with an average life-span of 79 years, make the call on which species will be harmful and which will remain benign in 10,000-year-old lakes?

Invasive species are often tougher and more adaptable, and lack natural predators in their newly invaded homes. Dreissenid mussels managed to survive a trip across the world sealed in a belly of a rusting ship, in complete darkness, with degraded oxygen. Then perhaps more remarkably, they survived a shocking transfer into a new environment. The ecological "bar" gets lower and lower as these hardened newcomers take over. Like weeds along a highway ditch, only the toughest few survive. Eventually the baseline quality of the lakes will become so low that no one will be able to fish or swim. A *balance* will be reached, but it will be an ever-expanding shift away from the Great Lakes that we know, and we need to decide if this is the balance we want.

Carp Threats

Finally, some invasive species are as sensational to look at as sea lampreys, are known to be ecologically destructive, like dreissenids, but have not yet made it into the Great Lakes. It is a rare case in which everyone agrees that these AIS are threats. Enter a bad family of invasive fishes, commonly grouped as "Asian carp," which have been on the brink of invading the Great Lakes for several years. There are four Asian carp species currently in the spotlight: silver carp (*Hypopthalmichthys molitrix*), bighead carp (*Hypopthalmichthys nobilis*), black carp (*Mylopharyngodon piceus*), and grass carp (*Ctenopharyngodon idella*). The threat of an Asian carp invasion in the Great Lakes has led to one of the most proactive and collaborative invasive species warning and prevention programs to date. The incentive to keep these AISs from entering

Dr. Seth Herbst, Aquatic Species and Regulatory Affairs unit manager with the Michigan DNR's Fisheries Division, holding a bighead carp. (Photo courtesy of Seth Herbst, Michigan Department of Natural Resources.)

the Great Lakes continues to grow. But will it be enough to deliver a wake-up call to policy makers that still don't recognize the threat?

Adult grass carp (*Ctenopharyngodon idella*), introduced in the United States in the 1960s to control weed growth in aquaculture ponds, have been found in Lakes Ontario, Erie, and Michigan already. Evidence of natural reproduction has been found in Lake Erie. Fisheries scientists and invasive species coordinators throughout the basin fear that the establishment of grass carp in the Great Lakes is inevitable within the next ten years.

Two of the four, the silver carp and bighead carp, originally introduced in Arkansas in the 1970s to control nutrients in aquaculture ponds, have spread through the Mississippi River basin and are currently at the brink of a Great Lakes invasion. They are held back solely by electrified barriers in Chicago shipping and sanitary canals. These two fish species, close cousins, are flat-out weird looking. Both species have down-set eyes and massive mouths, which make them appear alien. Silver carp overpopulate rivers to the point of crowding out other species and are known to spring out of the water when excited by the sound of motors. At 40 miles per hour, one could kill a person. Bighead carp can grow to the size of a German shepherd. Both species cruise through the water with wide-open mouths as they filter feed on phytoplankton and zooplankton.[10] Like invasive mussels, they eat away at the foundation of the food web.

On June 22, 2017, an eight-pound silver carp was caught in the Illinois River—just nine miles from Lake Michigan—during a routine monitoring mission upstream from an electrified barrier built to block them from the Great Lakes.[11] Each time silver carp get this close, alarm bells go off, newsfeeds erupt, and phone calls pour into policy makers' offices. The threat is clear thanks to decades of research focused on risk.

Mike Hoff, a retired fisheries biologist with the US Fish and Wildlife Service, dedicated his career to prevent silver and bighead carp from getting into the Great Lakes by developing a way to map and convey the risk associated with it actually happening. The Asian carp risk work that Mike spearheaded is currently part of one of the biggest international AIS prevention programs in the Great Lakes Basin. "There are four components of it," Mike explained in a low-slung voice over the phone: "*risk assessment*, which means to characterize risk; *risk management*, which means to attempt to minimize risk or eliminate it; *risk communication*, which describes the characterization of risk and the risk management actions that are undertaken or foregone; and *risk analysis*, which is a combination of risk assessment, risk management, and risk communication."

Mike knew from the beginning how important it is to stop these invaders. "These are a harmful species—we've got to keep them out of the Great Lakes." Now, more than a decade later, thanks to a tremendous collaborative effort by multiple state, federal, tribal, First Nation, and provincial agencies across the basin, the destructive potential of these fish is gin-clear to all. A growing understanding of the risk is creating an impetus to take action should they enter and establish,[12] which, many around the Great Lakes fear is inevitable.

The Great Lakes ecosystem, like a compromised immune system of a human body, is becoming increasingly less predictable, and we are only beginning to learn what types of environmental, economic, and health repercussions may come from it. Aquatic invasive species are acting like a virus in the Great Lakes. Some AISs, such as silver carp, create notice-able problems immediately; others, dreissenid mussels, are introduced, mostly ignored, and *incubate*. Without warning, maybe in 20 years, maybe in response to a disturbance like overfishing, a shift in weather patterns, climate change, habitat loss, another AIS, or pollution, an out-break could occur. Over the last century, human activity helped facilitate the introduction of more than 185 nonnative species around the Great Lakes, many of which are now considered invasive.[13]

Survival of the Fittest

Aquatic invasive species are tough as hell and adaptable, and this helps them thrive in a new environment. The fact that some can survive a transfer between freshwater and saltwater is physiologically astounding, though not exceptionally rare. Some fishes can adapt to live in fresh-water, some can only tolerate saltwater, some prefer brackish water (a mix of the two), and some can move between fresh and salt (e.g., most salmon species, sea lampreys, and American eels). A freshwater fish has a high concentration of salts inside its body compared to the outside water. Water continuously moves into the fish's body through the skin to equalize water and salt concentrations internally—a process known as osmoregulation. The kidneys work overtime to achieve this, and the fish pees a lot. A bonus is that it never has to drink. The opposite is true for marine fishes. Because of the salty ocean water, they constantly lose water from their less salty bodies. To compensate, they drink water around them and excrete extra salt from specialized cells in their gills. For these reasons, a bass from a backyard farm pond in Wisconsin would instantly die if tossed into the Atlantic Ocean. Likewise, a grouper caught in the ocean would die if plopped into the pond.

Other fishes, including sea lampreys, defy these physiological laws. As mentioned, sea lampreys are a marine species native to the Atlantic Ocean, where they are anadromous, which means they naturally detour from saltwater into freshwater tributary streams during their reproduc-tive or migratory stage. In their native range, adult sea lampreys histori-cally occurred along the Atlantic coast as far south as the St. Johns River in Florida and as far north as the mouth of the St. Lawrence River near Newfoundland.[14] They also ranged along the western coast of Europe.[15] Marine sea lampreys adapted to handle the physiological costs of mov-

ing between freshwater and saltwater. During their freshwater transformation from larvae to adult, sea lampreys develop gills with specialized
cells involved in osmoregulation, along with tough skin that secretes a
protective slime layer. These adaptations allow them to deal with the
constant water loss and high salinity on entering the ocean.[16]

A big question remains. How did a marine fish get into the lakes in
the first place? Whether sea lampreys are actually native to Lake Ontario
or not has been relentlessly debated by researchers since the 1970s.
Extensive historical research by fisheries biologist Randy Eshenroder, a
longtime expert on the subject with the Great Lakes Fishery Commission in Ann Arbor, suggests a nonnative classification of sea lampreys in
Lakes Ontario and Champlain. "I was in Syracuse, New York, and I was
going through the Erie Canal Museum," Randy mentioned in his Ann
Arbor office. "Up in an attic in a back area I saw this very, very large map
of the Erie Canal."

Randy explained that the old map showed the locations of all of the
man-made ditches, connections, and modifications made during the
early Erie Canal construction period. "I could stand back and actually
follow the markers that showed the way they [the lampreys] got in," he
said. He had connected the dots, literally, and discovered several locations of canal-related engineering mishaps in the mid-1800s that would
have created a direct path through which sea lampreys could enter.
Randy discovered that there were watershed breaches beginning in 1863
between the Susquehanna River drainage.[17] Breaches also occurred at
several locations throughout the Lake Ontario drainage basin, including
the Oswego River drainage.[18] Sea lampreys would have had new access
to spawning habitat above Oneida Lake, and newly transformed sea
lampreys could then have moved down and dropped over a man-made
spillway into Oneida Lake. From there access to Lake Ontario would
have been a straight shot.[19]

But the canal breach data doesn't convince everyone. One could
argue that sea lampreys have had access to Lake Ontario since the Great
Lakes were formed. Atlantic salmon (*Salmo salar*) were native to Lake
Ontario until they were wiped out through habitat loss and overfishing
by 1890. If salmon that originated in the Atlantic Ocean were native to
Lake Ontario thousands of years ago, Atlantic sea lampreys could have
come along for the ride—perhaps literally. American eels, which are
native to Lake Ontario yet migrate to the Atlantic Ocean to reproduce,

Lake Ontario and the Finger Lakes of New York showing possible invasion points (*stars*) for a sea lamprey invasion into the Finger Lakes and Lake Ontario. (Adapted from Eshenroder, "Role of the Champlain Canal.") The small inset map shows the sea lamprey's native North American range (*shaded diagonal lines*) and invasive range (*shaded gray*). (Adapted from the USGS via https://nas.er.usgs.gov/queries/factsheet. aspx?SpeciesID=836) (Map by author, not to scale.)

have been moving between the two through the St. Lawrence River for centuries.

Sea lampreys would have had a chance to become isolated in Lake Ontario roughly 6,000 years ago, around the time of the St. Lawrence embayment. Concluding Earth's most recent period of repeated glaciation known as the Pleistocene Epoch, which lasted roughly 2.5 million years and ended a mere 11,700 years ago, glaciers receded from the ancient geologic depression that is now drained by the St. Lawrence River. The receding glaciers created a temporary inlet to the Atlantic Ocean known as the Champlain Sea. This salty arm of the Atlantic Ocean covered parts of Quebec and Ontario, as well as what is now Upstate New York and Vermont. Beginning roughly 9,500 years ago, gradual continental uplift allowed the expanse of seawater to drain back into the Atlantic Ocean. For the next 3,500 years, extensive drainage carved the St. Lawrence River into an artery that drains the Great Lakes Basin. It is possible that an inland population of sea lampreys was left stranded to lurk in the newly created freshwater of Lake Ontario.[20]

The wide range of names given to sea lampreys makes it difficult to find early reports related to their history in Lake Ontario. When early reports are discovered, it is nearly impossible to determine which species of lamprey is described, or if it is a lamprey at all. Even today, sea lampreys are mistakenly referred to as eels, although they are not related. Larval sea lampreys have been called mud-eels, mud lampreys, or sand lampreys. Adults have been called eels, great sea lampreys, river lampreys, green lampreys, lake lampreys, shad lampreys, lamprey-eels, lamper-eels, lamphrey-eels, suckers, and of course *nine-eyes*.[21]

Early Pests

Taken together it seems fairly clear that sea lampreys in Lake Ontario have been correctly given a nonnative classification. The timeline of Eshenroder's breaches matches the first reports of sea lamprey damage in the Lake Ontario Basin. Just a few years after the 1863 canal breach, a graduate student at Cornell University named Simon H. Gage was directed by his advisor, Professor Burt G. Wilder, to study "land-locked sea lampreys" of the connecting Oneida and Cayuga lakes, just a few miles from Lake Ontario's shores.[22]

In an ironic twist, sea lampreys in their native North American range suffered a population decline by the 1880s. Sea lampreys have been a culinary delicacy all the way back to the Romans of the first and second centuries. Early European settlement along the eastern US coast brought with it many traditions, including the catching, cooking, and eating of sea lampreys. Lampreys are the key ingredient in the Queen's Jubilee pie—a tradition that goes as far back as the Middle Ages. Even today marine-run sea lampreys from various rivers in southeastern Europe are considered a delicacy. Dams, pollution, and exploitation added to their decline. In 1882 the Connecticut legislature introduced a law "for the protection of lamprey eels in the Connecticut River" near Hartford, Connecticut. In an article published in *The Day* on March 3, 1882, it was reported that the bill to protect sea lampreys during their spawning run was rejected in the state Senate the day before, having been previously passed by the House. Several years later "House Bill 207" established a season for harvesting sea lampreys in Connecticut, which only allowed sea lampreys to be taken from April 1 to May 20 in the Farmington, Connecticut, and Scantic Rivers.[23] Around the same time, just a few hundred miles to the northwest, reports of damage by "land-locked sea lampreys" began to emerge.

By the 1890s, Gage and Wilder had made considerable discoveries regarding the life cycle and feeding habits of the "lake" sea lampreys. At this point Gage was a professor at Cornell with his own graduate student, H. A. Surface. Surface issued a warning about the destructive nature of sea lampreys during his studies. He referred to sea lampreys as "lake lampreys" in Cayuga Lake, believed to be a subspecies of *Petromyzon marinus*. Wilder, Gage, and Surface named the lake lampreys *Petromyzon marinus unicolor* based on their smaller body size and more uniform coloration during the spawning season. Actually these were just sea lampreys adapted to a fully freshwater life, and they were turning bullheads (*Ameiurus nebulosus*) into Swiss cheese.

Bullheads were one of the only species still abundant after nearly a century of heavy fishing pressure in the Finger Lakes. Surface estimated that roughly 500,000 pounds were placed on the market annually from these New York lakes alone. Bullheads were big business.

Surface spent the spring of 1897 wandering the shores of Cayuga Lake with a long net called a seine that he and an assistant would drag through the shallows to catch bullheads. He quickly found that it was easy to spot the bullheads that had been attacked by lampreys, "even when they were purposely turned over so that the holes were not visible." He noted, "The injured fish loses entirely its rich golden hue, and, assuming a sickly appearance, grows paler and weaker." He had discovered in his graduate studies that twelve out of every fifteen bullheads caught "had been attacked by lampreys."[24]

People's understanding of the destructive potential of sea lampreys was growing in Lake Ontario. In 1891 C. W. Nash of Toronto wrote in his field notebook that fishes in Toronto Bay, on the north shore of Lake Ontario, were "suffering terribly from the attacks of lampreys." Nash noted that walleye, northern pike, whitefish, black bass, and suckers were also floating dead in the bay with lamprey scars: "Many fine fish are to be seen floating about the bay killed in this fashion, and very few are

Photographs by H. A. Surface in 1897 showing brown bullheads "fatally attacked" by landlocked sea lampreys in Cayuga Lake, New York. Surface also described "The body wall being entirely cut through by these blood-suckers, and the abdominal cavity penetrated." Surface's "lake lampreys" turned out to be sea lampreys. (H. A. Surface, *The Lampreys of Central New York* [New York: National Fishery Congress Bulletin of the United States Fishery Commission, 1897], plates 10 and 11.)

caught that do not show marks of having suffered from a more or less prolonged visit of this wretched parasite, two or three holes being found in some cases."[25] Professor Gage began regularly publishing details about the feeding habits, destructive behavior, and life history of the land-locked sea lamprey.[26] Nash continued reporting damage near Toronto. "Saw another lake trout washed up today evidently killed by a lamprey," he wrote as he walked along the beach near east Toronto in 1899. "I must have found a dozen this winter along the beach killed in this manner."[27]

Scarred fish and sea lamprey sightings were not commonly reported in Lake Ontario prior to the 1880s, perhaps for a number of reasons. Lake Ontario historically supported the smallest commercial fishing industry in the Great Lakes, which was the main way to observe lamprey destruction. The commercially important species in Lake Ontario at the time included yellow perch, whitefish, bullheads, and American eels.[28] These species are smaller than lake trout on average and are not likely to survive an attack long enough to exhibit scars. Habitat was degraded, even for sea lampreys. The tributary streams that ran into Lake Ontario, and the rest of the Great Lakes for that matter, were used as conveyer belts during the logging days, moving masses of logs downstream to be loaded onto barges. Logjams chewed away fish-spawning habitat. Deforestation around historically tree-shaded streams caused undercut banks to collapse, channels to widen, and streams to become warm. Dams caused the once swift and cold stream water to slow and drop sediment loads onto gravel spawning grounds. All of these factors would keep sea lamprey populations low.

While water from Lake Erie has always flowed into Lake Ontario via the Niagara River, fish passage from Lake Ontario to Lake Erie, as well as ship passage, was historically barred by thundering 167-foot-high Niagara Falls. In 1825 the Erie Canal was completed after just eight years of construction. The 360-mile-long shipping canal connecting the Hudson River at Albany, New York, to Lake Erie at Buffalo, New York, went from being sarcastically referred to as a ditch to being described as an engineering marvel by the mid-nineteenth century. Just four years later the Welland Canal was completed. The Welland Canal also connects Lake Ontario to Lake Erie but in a 27-mile straight shot that bypasses Niagara Falls just a few miles to the west. Ships could now push their way into the upper Great Lakes.

If ships could make it from Lake Ontario to Lake Erie, fishes could too. At this point in the story it becomes important to step back and briefly discuss the connectivity of the Great Lakes. Some refer to the Great Lakes as one big "river." They've always been a flowing, dynamic system, but hundreds of years of building canals, locks, and diversions now allow 1,000-foot freighters to move freely among them. A person can now travel from the Caribbean Gulf of Mexico, up the Mississippi River, through the Great Lakes, and eventually reach the Atlantic Ocean, all by water. Lake Michigan is connected to the Mississippi River via the Chicago Sanitary and Ship Canal. Lake Huron shares shifting currents with Lake Michigan under the towering Mackinac Bridge through the Straits of Mackinac. Lake Superior, the largest of the five Great Lakes, flows into Lake Huron via the St. Marys River and the Soo Locks at Sault Ste. Marie. To the south, Lake Huron drains into the channelized St. Clair River, through Lake St. Clair, the Detroit River, and eventually meets Lake Erie. Lake Erie water flows through the Niagara River where it crashes over Niagara Falls, or flows lazily through the Welland Shipping Canal bypassing Niagara Falls, eventually reaching Lake Ontario. The St. Lawrence River drains Lake Ontario, flows past Montreal and Québec City, and mixes with the Atlantic Ocean at the Gulf of the St. Lawrence. In summary, once an organism has access to Lake Erie, it has access to the entire Great Lakes basin.

The Welland Canal was modified repeatedly in response to growing North American industries by the early twentieth century. In the years leading up to World War I, demands for shipping increased exponentially and a complete overhaul was under way by 1913. Major modifications completed by 1919 diverted new water sources into the canal, widened channels, and caused water to flow in a uniform direction from Lake Erie into Lake Ontario. Wooden Great Lakes steam ships hundreds of feet long could now move back and forth between Lakes Ontario to Erie with ease. While no one knew it at the time, widening the Welland Canal would turn out to be perhaps the biggest ecological mishap of the twentieth century.

Two years later, on November 8, 1921, Mr. Alexander Crewe of the Crewe Brothers Fishery was lifting his pound nets loaded with fish a few miles out from Merlin, Ontario, in Lake Erie. The nets were around 150 nautical miles west of the Welland Canal connection to Lake Ontario. That day he noticed something strange. Thrashing in a net was a 21-inch-long snakelike creature attached to one of his whitefish. Crewe would have encountered native lampreys before in his 25-plus years on these waters but never anything this size. The specimen was dropped into a jar and sent to the University of Toronto, where experts confirmed it was a parasitic sea lamprey. Crewe had reported the first sea lamprey ever found in Lake Erie. Professor John R. Dymond of the University of Toronto zoology department briefly acknowledged the specimen in his 1922 publication "A Provisional List of the Fishes of Lake Erie," but no alarm bells rang.[29]

Sea lamprey populations were beginning to climb in Lake Ontario at the time of the first Lake Erie sighting in November 1921. Dymond and his colleague A. F. Coventry were leading authorities on sea lampreys at the University of Toronto, having studied them in Lake Ontario for several years at this point. Earlier in 1921, Dymond had received multiple reports from anglers that sea lampreys were being taken in the Humber River, a tributary to Lake Ontario, attached to suckers.[30] In May, Dymond began to make regular trips to the Humber River just west of Toronto to observe the hundreds of spawning sea lampreys that would accumulate below the Lambton weir, a low-head dam that spanned the entire length of the river. During his trips, he noted that these lampreys "appeared to be blocked in their ascent of the stream by the weir, which is about three feet high."[31] Observations like Dymond's would eventually inform the first sea lamprey control program spearheaded by Cliff Kortman and Vernon Applegate in the upper lakes a few decades later.

CHAPTER 2

THE DECK OF THE *BEATRICE M*

The sea lamprey invasion in the upper Great Lakes happened slowly and in the shadows of three major pillars of North American history—World War I, the Great Depression, and World War II. Sea lampreys were now in Lake Erie and had free rein to spread through the entire Great Lakes. It would be another six years, in 1927, before the next sea lamprey would be confirmed in Lake Erie. This one was confirmed by John Van Oosten during his first year as director of the US Bureau of Fisheries Great Lakes lab in Ann Arbor. Van Oosten's discovery worried him. New creatures had shown up in nets previously in the Great Lakes, but something about this one was different.

A few years later, on October 28, 1929, the Wall Street crash ushered in the Great Depression—a worldwide economic crisis that lasted well into the 1930s. Sightings of sea lampreys popped up over the next decade: a parasitic adult near Point Aux Pins, Ontario, and one near Sandusky, Ohio, in 1928; a parasitic adult in the St. Clair River near Detroit in 1930; spawning adults in the Huron River in Wayne County, Michigan, in 1932; spawning adults in Swan Creek, a tributary of the Maumee River near Toledo, Ohio, in 1934 and 1935; and a few more around Lake Erie's western basin.[1]

Then a specimen was confirmed in Lake Michigan near Milwaukee in 1936. As a boat sails, this was nearly 700 miles away from the previous sightings near Sandusky. No one knows how the jump happened. It's likely that sea lampreys were seen in Lake Huron but not reported. Some thought the parasite may have been brought from the lower lakes in a bucket and released. Others argued that it was the popularity of larval sea lampreys for bait that allowed the spread to move through the Great Lakes in an unpredictable way. Regardless, the sea lamprey invasion took the residents of the upper Great Lakes Basin by surprise by the late 1930s.

Commercial fishing gill net tugs sit idle in a harbor in Erie, Pennsylvania, in September 1928. (Photo courtesy of the John Van Oosten Library, US Geological Survey.)

Sea lampreys are known for their hitchhiking abilities, and it may have helped them move around the Great Lakes. In the October 4, 1888, issue of *Forest and Stream* a story ran regarding sea lampreys hitching rides on the rudder of a yacht, which apparently gave the captain a fright.[2] In 1922, A. F. Coventry of the Department of Biology, University of Toronto, published a key paper titled "Breeding Habits of the Land-Locked Sea Lamprey," which would serve as one of the earliest references for sea lamprey behavior in the Great Lakes. He states, "For many years it has been known locally that a lamprey occurs in Lake Ontario at least some miles east and west of Toronto, where it is sometimes greatly in evidence, attaching itself temporarily to boats in motion or more especially to food-fishes and thus brought up by fishermen operating gill nets for whitefish and lake trout in the open waters."[3]

While sea lampreys never actually attack people, they attached to swimmers from time to time at the peak of the lamprey infestation. One of the earliest reports occurred in Lake Ontario when a large group of open water swimmers and escort boats found "large lampreys" attached to them during a 21-mile race in August 1927. Another report emerged when a sea lamprey hitched a ride on Vivian Lee Walsh during the Wrigley Ten-Mile Swim for Women in 1929. Walsh was among 45 competitors in the swim, which took place in the Toronto harbor with a prize of 10,000 dollars. More than 100,000 spectators showed up, all of whom watched the Olympic athlete Martha Norelius take the lead from the start and maintain it for a record-breaking win. Most of the swimmers could barely move in the freezing water. An article stated, "Miss Walsh suffered an added horror when she encountered a lamprey eel. She freed herself from the eel after a frenzied battle, but was immediately seized with cramps and chills."[4] Near Harbor Springs, Michigan, in the 1950s, 13-year-old Edith Juilleret was in the middle of a three-quarter-mile qualification swim in Lake Michigan for her Red Cross lifesaving certificate when a sea lamprey reportedly attached to her foot. This particular sea lamprey encounter gets infinitely more interesting. Her father, Earl, pulled her out of the water and claimed that it was probably karma: "A sea lamprey got even with a former commercial fisherman after carrying a family grudge for almost 19 years." Earl Juilleret claimed he had caught and reported the first sea lamprey in Lake Michigan in 1934, and the lampreys finally got even.[5]

Commercial fishers on the lakes were the first to experience the worst of the sea lampreys, and they were the first to react. Beatrice Skaggs (née Mertz) was raised just up the road from Cliff Kortman, and has strong memories of her first experiences with sea lampreys. "Well we knew they were destructive by just looking at the mouth of the lamprey and seeing it suction," Bea said in her home near Cheboygan, Michigan. Bea comes from a long line of strong-willed commercial fishers. Her paternal grandmother, Mary Mertz, owned part of the commercial fishery in Rogers City, Michigan, around the turn of the century. By 1911 Bea's father Louis and her uncles Clarence and Lawrence all worked as fishermen in the family business. Louis also worked at a calcite quarry in Rogers City to save money so he could one day fish full time.

Most kids born into fishing families were riding along in a net box on the fishing boats before they could walk. "I can remember my dad, I was only four but I can still picture my dad sitting at the table telling us about the lamprey coming into the Great Lakes, and he kept telling us that it was going to be an evil thing," Bea said as she recalled one of her few memories of her father. Bea was just a toddler when her family received the news that Louis had become entangled in fishing gear and drowned while fishing off of Harbor Beach, Michigan, in June 1934.

At the rock bottom of the Great Depression, Bea's mother Kather-

Louis Mertz proudly holds up a nice lake trout at the Rogers City harbor in 1921.
(Photo courtesy Beatrice Skaggs.)

ine took over the fishing business. She hired a crew and fished out of Rogers City for the next several years. The family fished with eight deep-water trap nets, setting and checking them with a boat fittingly named the *Beatrice M*. The trap nets were a new technology that allowed fishing in deeper water compared to the shallower pound, or "pond," nets, which were anchored in the shallows and supported with wooden poles pounded into the sediment. In both types of nets, fish were still alive when brought up to the boat. Bea's family primarily targeted whitefish. These Great Lakes natives have flaky white flesh and a mild flavor—they are a delicacy. Live fish trapped in a net are an easy target for sea lampreys, and Bea's family was one of the first to learn this.

"I was just a youngster, and my job was to cut up the lampreys that came in on whitefish," Bea chuckled while thumbing through old family photos. "I kept saying to my mom, "I don't want to do this." She said, "You can't put it back in there alive," so I learned how to use the knife." Bea explained that this was her job on the deck of the *Beatrice M* as a kid in the early 1940s, along with guiding the waterlogged nets into the scow (a small boat) from the Lake Huron depths. "I remember so distinctly my first experience with taking a snakelike creature and cutting its head off. That was quite an experience. But, I got to be pretty proficient at it," Bea added.

Fishing families saw a problem and immediately reacted. The health of the fishery and their livelihoods were connected—a threat to fishes was a threat to the family. Commercial fishers in Bea's generation never forgot how bad the sea lamprey infestation was. As if 70 years ago were yesterday, Bea mentioned that she still had the old fish knife that "cut a lot of lamprey."

Bea spent most of her summers before high school on the boats lifting nets and beheading lampreys until her mother retired and sold the business in 1947. "My mother was the boss, and we worked under her. She taught us a lot," Bea told me. As Bea puts it about her mother best, "She was a lady ahead of her time." Clearly so is Bea.

Beas family wasn't pushed out of business by the sea lampreys—they just narrowly dodged that bullet. Instead, Bea's mother kept the fishing business afloat through family tragedy, the Great Depression, World War II, and the first wave of lamprey attacks. And she made enough to retire comfortably.

Families Like Bea's, and hundreds more around the basin, represent

Alfred Basel carries a nice lake trout caught in a Mertz Fishery deep trap net. Beatrice Mertz is on the right. (Photo courtesy Beatrice Skaggs.)

a commercial fishing community that generated steam to do something about sea lampreys. But they weren't the only ones impacted. While it's rarely written about, there was still a very prominent sport fishery on the Great Lakes back then.

Heading up the rocky north shore of Lake Superior on Highway 61, about 20 miles north of Duluth, Minnesota, you pass a dirt turnoff you would ordinarily never notice. Down at the shoreline there remain a few weathered chunks of concrete among the wave-pounded rocks, along with some steel posts. This was once Bluebird Landing, a Great Lakes sport-fishing resort.

"I was born in 1941," Mary Ann Sironen said in her home near Duluth. Mary Ann's friends Merle Norgren and Stuart Sivertson, both retired Lake Superior commercial fishermen from the area, joined us at the table.[6] "We grew up with Bluebird Landing in its heyday," she said.

Mary Ann's parents, Tim Lukkonen and Evelyn Sandberg Lukkonen, started the resort with a 1,000-dollar loan and a dream to bring a "deep

(*Top photo*): Katherine Mertz pauses from working with the Bell Brother's Fishery in Cheboygan, Michigan, c. 1940. (Photo used with permission from the History Center of Cheboygan and Ross Bell of Cheboygan, Michigan.) (*Bottom photo*): Sea gulls pick a fish box clean on the deck of the wooden trap net boat *Beatrice M*, the same deck where sea lamprey heads rolled under Bea's knife, as it cruises back from the fishing grounds c. 1940. (Photo courtesy of Beatrice Skaggs.)

The "deep-sea fishing" adventures and life at Bluebird Landing, an early Great Lakes sport-fishing resort that once boomed along the north shore of Lake Superior near Duluth, Minnesota. (Photos courtesy of Mary Ann Sironen.)

sea fishing experience" to the Midwest. "There were a lot of [sport-fishing resorts] around back then," Mary Ann said as she recalled her mother's fresh pies at the Landing's train-car diner and running around the resort docks as a kid.

A sport-fishing outing on the Great Lakes was an event: a sport coat and tie, fancy hat event. After World War II, more families had the expendable income to take trips, go camping, and enjoy cruises, resorts, and fishing adventures on the Great Lakes. People wanted to catch big lake trout.

Sea lampreys "probably came in the later 1940s," Merle noted. He also remarked that Bluebird supplemented its income in the off-season with a commercial fishing operation, and that he had often worked the nets on the family gill net tug *Blue Jay*. "First we started seeing [scars] on fish," Merle said, "so we knew something was happening." "The first sea

BlueBird Landing as seen from Lake Superior

BlueBird Landing as seen from North Shore Drive

BlueBird Landing

DEEP SEA   FISHING

IN   LAKE   SUPERIOR

Also Boat Rides -- 5 Mile Ride for $1.00 per person

14 miles from downtown Duluth
on the scenic North Shore Drive

BlueBird Landing, North Shore Drive, Duluth 4, Minn.

The original Bluebird Landing flyer. (Courtesy Mary Ann Sironen.)

lamprey I saw was in a pickle jar, and it had sucked onto the side of the glass with its big *ishy* mouth," Mary Ann added.

Mary Ann recalled that everyone who fished along the north shore of Lake Superior from Minnesota through Ontario remembers seeing sea lampreys for the first time: "People thought they were like horrible creatures from the bottom of the earth because they were so unfamiliar to us—we hadn't seen that kind of a thing come out of the water before."

Sea lampreys began to hurt business almost immediately. Still, Mary Ann told me that her dad didn't think it was just sea lampreys destroying the trout and distressing customers: "Dad thought that the smelt ate the lake trout fry, so that also contributed to the downfall of the trout."

Mary Ann's mother Evelyn wrote an article about the rise and fall of Bluebird Landing with Alvera Pierson in 1971, and Mary Ann showed me a copy of her mom's work. Toward the middle of the article, two excerpts struck me.

Sport fishing on Lake Superior reached its height in the late '40s and early '50s, then became less and less each year. Everyone kept talking about the lamprey that had invaded the Great Lakes. . . .

No one had any idea just how soon the lamprey would deplete the trout. Many lake trout caught during this period would either have a lamprey attached or it would have the lamprey scar showing that it had survived the attack of the predator.[7]

While reading the article and chatting at the table, Mary Ann, Merle, and Stuart pointed out that another environmental blow came in the form of tens of thousands of pounds of taconite tailings, a by-product of extracting low-grade iron ore from rock, that were dumped directly into Lake Superior just up the shore by the Reserve Mining Company in the mid-1950s.[8]

Stuart explained that the tailings "changed the color of the water, extended out in a plume from the shoreline," and almost immediately "the fishermen in the downstream of this plume no longer got any cisco." The dense slurry of fine-particle tailings disrupted midwater and benthic feeding grounds and smothered spawning reefs in tandem with sea lampreys' destruction of adult whitefish and trout, a combination of an AIS and pollution that ultimately laid their fishing business, and many others' in the area, to rest.

Fishing families around the basin began to consider overfishing as a cause of local fish collapses by the mid-1930s. Others argued that it was natural for populations of certain species to fluctuate. Sea lampreys went from mostly unheard of to the "scourge of Great Lakes fishes" in less than a decade. The headline ran "Dread Sea Lampreys in First Spawn Run" in the August 15, 1937, edition of the *Milwaukee Journal* after hundreds of sex-crazed sea lampreys were found lined up like cordwood at a popular swimming hole in none other than Michigan's Ocqueoc River— referred to as "the falls." The spectacle was reported by Conservation

A Michigan Department of Conservation officer hoists a dip net full of sea lampreys out of the Ocqueoc River barrier trap near the Highway 23 Bridge, Millersburg, Michigan, c. 1940s. (Photo courtesy of the John Van Oosten Library, US Geological Survey.)

Left, emptying deepwater trap nets aboard the *Beatrice M* in 1939; *right*, the Mertz Fishery crew and the *Beatrice M* up on the ice. (Photos courtesy of Beatrice Skaggs.)

Officer Marvin L. Norton in his semimonthly report for the Michigan Department of Conservation.[9] Officer Norton grabbed two specimens from nests near the falls after "two Rogers City boys" who had been swimming about a quarter mile downstream reported "hundreds of eels in the river." After pulling a few off of the rocks at the falls, it was quickly realized that these were not eels.

At the same time, Bea's uncle, Clarence Mertz, noted that catches of lake trout in 1937 were dropping in Lake Huron's Hammond Bay. The trout he was able to catch often had strange ulcers on their sides. Clarence informed Dr. John Van Oosten, director of the US Bureau of Fisheries Great Lakes Fishery lab in Ann Arbor, that four of every five lake trout he took during his June fishing season that year were scarred. By August Clarence had caught about 30 sea lampreys fishing out of Rogers City. Given the animal's life history, catching 30 parasitic-phase sea lampreys in just a few months, along with the presence of a large adult spawning run in the Ocqueoc River that spring, suggests sea lampreys were already in northern Lake Huron several years earlier.

The presence of the spawning run at the Ocqueoc River falls reaffirmed concerns across the basin that an invasion was happening. The spark of a potential sea lamprey problem in the Great Lakes had flickered farther south a year earlier when the first parasitic-phase sea lamprey was confirmed in Lake Michigan near Milwaukee. On March 23, 1936, Captain Frank C. Paczocha brought a 16-inch "eellike" fish to the Milwaukee Public Museum along with a lot of head-scratching questions. Paczocha mentioned that the sea lamprey was attached "just below the eye" on a 4.5-pound lake trout he caught while fishing 15 miles east of Milwaukee in Lake Michigan. T. E. B. Pope, curator of lower zoology at the Milwaukee Public Museum, knew right away that this wasn't a native lamprey. Pope issued the first public warning about the dangers of this new predator in the upper Great Lakes: "It will be well if all commercial fishermen and lovers of game fishes will kill at sight any of these parasitic, destructive fish."[10]

The story of Captain Frank's catch made the Wisconsin and Michigan newspapers. It was also published in a popular fishing industry newspaper, *The Fisherman*.[11] Pope continued writing after seeing the parasite in the flesh. On August 27, 1936, he released a bulletin for the American Fisheries Society titled "The Spread of the Sea Lamprey through the Great Lakes." In this report, coauthored with Carl Hubbs, a world-renowned researcher of fishes at the University of Michigan, the two issued a public warning about the impending invasion. There weren't a lot of control or eradication suggestions in the early report. Instead, Hubbs and Pope advised, "For the present, attempts to control this unwanted and destructive immigrant into the Great Lakes waters would seem practicably limited to the killing of all individuals caught by fishermen."[12] This article, and other media buzz, inspired fishing outfits like the Mertz's to take action and destroy as many sea lampreys as possible.

Back in Ann Arbor, John Van Oosten had been on edge about the impending sea lamprey invasion for years. Reports of sea lamprey sightings continued to pour in from commercial fishers. Van Oosten worked closely with Fred A. Westerman, who was chief of the Michigan Department of Conservation's Fisheries Division from 1925 to 1959. They were both in the same cohort of early Great Lakes fishery scientists. More important, both understood that the best way to get vital information regarding the spread of sea lampreys would be from the commercial fishers of the lakes—the people who were experiencing the damage firsthand. Westerman and Van Oosten worried about sea lampreys entering Lake Superior, which was now the last stronghold of an endemic population of lake trout. They would set out regularly to interview members of the commercial fishing industry to collect data.

Fred A. Westerman (*left*) and John Van Oosten (*right*) stand on a dock with a gill net tug moored behind them during one of their interview trips, c. 1940s. (Photo by Carlos Fetterolf, courtesy of the Great Lakes Fishery Commission.)

The two happened to embark on one such research excursion in November 1937. All that was keeping sea lampreys from Lake Superior at this time was a straight shot through the St. Marys River, a 75-mile connection that steadily flows southeast as it drains Lake Superior into northern Lake Huron. The shores of Lake Superior throughout Ontario, Michigan, Wisconsin, and Minnesota were wild and remote at the time. Dirt roads branched through dense forests if there was any road at all. The two researchers tracked down various commercial-fishing ports consisting of some rickety old docks and tippy fish houses along Lake Superior's southern shore. In 27 pages of detailed field notes on their interviews with more than 20 commercial fishermen, lampreys were mentioned only twice. The first came when the two interviewed the proprietor of Hill and Son Fisheries. The notes relate, "Hill says he has seen no sea lampreys except the small one which is occasionally taken." Hill went on to say that "this is perhaps the native species."[13]

The other report came on November 24 in Munising, Michigan, when the two interviewed a few unnamed fishermen at H. E. Anderson and Sons. They reported that lake trout had been depleted to the point that they rarely caught any. The owner, H. E. Anderson, saw his first lamprey ever that summer attached to a lake trout. "The lamprey was about 8 inches long," he said. Van Oosten and Westerman passed it off as a native lamprey as well. Reports of native lamprey sightings that were thought to be sea lampreys were common around this time. Fishing families reported that smelt, which had been around this area for the past three springs, and fishing pressure were mainly to blame for the spotty lake trout catches in southern Lake Superior.[14]

On March 13, 1938, the headline "Marine World Villain Preys on Great Lakes" ran in local newspapers referring to the sea lampreys' impending invasion of Lake Superior.[15] In the article, Van Oosten warned that sea lampreys were spreading rapidly through the Great Lakes. Sea lampreys were regularly caught near the Straits of Mackinac, and "it wouldn't be long until they made it into Superior." Van Oosten's words were a harbinger of what was to come.

A few months later that year, predictably, a sea lamprey was confirmed in Lake Superior for the first time just a few miles from the area Van Oosten and Westerman had visited the previous year. News of the sea lamprey caught in Lake Superior near Marquette, Michigan, was reported in a 1938 edition of the *Marquette Daily Mining Journal*.[16] Over the next few years, reports of sea lamprey sightings began to pop up around Lake Superior as residents continued to follow news about the devastation they were causing in the remaining fishery in the lower lakes.

By the mid-1940s, sea lampreys were established throughout the entire Great Lakes. But the damage was still variable across the basin. Some areas, such as northern Lakes Huron and Michigan, were infested to the extent that up to 80% of commercially caught fishes were wounded and "not salable." Fish throughout most of Lake Erie and the north shore of Lake Superior were still relatively unscathed. Confirmation of the spotty sea lamprey distribution came in 1947 when a bounty was placed on its head by the Stone Laboratory of Ohio State University, located on Gibraltar Island in western Lake Erie. The crew at Stone Lab offered commercial fishers a one-dollar reward for each sea lamprey turned in

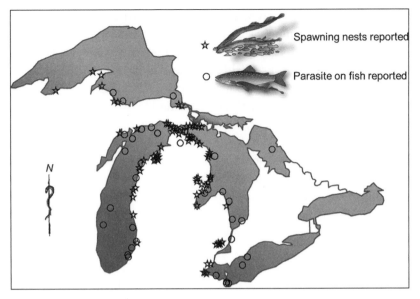

Locations of sea lamprey sightings during surveys conducted by Shetter in 1947 and Applegate in 1950. (Map by author, not to scale.)

that year. Only one sea lamprey was brought in by "a fishermen who has been commercially fishing since about 1920." With the report there is another curious note: "It was the first sea lamprey he had ever seen."

This isn't to say sea lamprey reports *never* came from Lake Erie in the late 1940s. One fisherman reported to the Ohio Conservation Department that he took 38 pounds of blue pike and 1,495 pounds of "herring" in Lake Erie.[17] He included a note: "There are a few lamper-eel after the herring—have to let the herring go. There is an open sore on the side of quite a lot of fish!"[18]

The feeling among commercial fishers throughout the basin ranged from slightly concerned to full-on panicked, with no recognizable pattern to determine who would be impacted by the invader next. The spread had to be mapped. But just as plans were being made, all resources were diverted—this time by World War II.

In Toronto, on March 7, 1945, the Department of Game and Fisheries Fish Culture Branch drafted a survey asking license-holding commercial fishing operations to report sea lampreys and scarring, focusing primarily on the worst areas: Georgian Bay and the North Channel of Lake Huron. In Michigan, Dr. David S. Shetter, an associate aquatic biologist at the University of Michigan Institute for Fisheries Research, had been recording sea lamprey sightings in the upper Great Lakes starting as early as 1943. Shetter's goal was to map the presence of sea lamprey spawning runs throughout Michigan waters of the Great Lakes. Questionnaires were sent to license-holding commercial fishers in an early attempt to map the locations of the infestation.

In response to the surveys, sea lamprey spawning runs were reported as far south as the St. Clair River and as far north as the tip of the Keweenaw Peninsula. By the time the surveys wrapped up in 1946, several key lessons had been learned as a battle against sea lampreys in the Great Lakes brewed on the horizon.

- An allocation of resources was needed to fund scientific research on sea lamprey control.
- Although sea lampreys were found throughout the lakes, they weren't found spawning in every tributary, which might provide an advantage.
- There were two vulnerable stages in the sea lampreys' life cycle, migratory and larval, which could be exploited by new control methods.
- Cross-border cooperation was the only option if the fishery was to be saved.

CHAPTER 3

NATIONS ARE JOLTED TO ACTION

The attitude of the people toward scientific investigation of the fisheries
has undergone a distinct change in the last five years. While the tendency
was noticeable many years before, it has been only very recently that we
find dealers and fishermen, leaders of the industry, advocating fishery
regulation, requesting technical advice, and calling upon us to draft
appropriate legislation to protect the fisheries.

—HENRY O'MALLEY, 1927

The gruesome sight of sea lamprey damage on commercially important
fishes finally awakened Canada and the United States to the dire state
of the Great Lakes fishery. It was a wake-up call that saved a few species from extinction. For centuries the fish supply of the Great Lakes
was considered limitless. From the Industrial Revolution through World
War I, demands on natural resources eroded all conservation or scientific efforts. Then in the middle of the 1920s, without warning, the
fishery of Lake Erie crashed. Commercial fishing companies were in an
uproar. Everyone blamed everyone else. The situation escalated to where
environmental officials from the states and the province of Ontario bordering Lake Erie were forced to come together to discuss fisheries management issues on the Great Lakes. On January 4–7, 1927, a meeting
was held to discuss the disaster in Lake Erie. It was the first meeting of
the Division of Scientific Inquiry,[1] and the first Great Lakes divisional
conference of the US Bureau of Fisheries, the predecessor to the US Fish
and Wildlife Service.

Walter Koelz, an early Great Lakes fisheries scientist with the US
Bureau of Fisheries, had been studying whitefish and cisco in Lake
Huron for a number of years during his graduate work at the University
of Michigan. He was one of the few at the time who understood how
depleted the fishery was. Each lake historically contained a distinctive
forage base consisting of several unique morphotypes, and perhaps a few

separate species, of native deepwater cisco (*Coregonus spp.*). The exact number of species and morphotypes of cisco that existed in each lake are still under debate today. From 1919 to 1920, Koelz captured more than 3,000 cisco specimens from Lake Huron during one of the first Great Lakes population studies. In a 1920 report of the Progress in Biological Inquiries, Koelz wrote about his extensive cisco research. He claimed there were 10 forms of cisco in the Great Lakes, 8 species and 2 subspecies, all of which are referred to the Linnaean genus *Coregonus*. Over the century leading up to Koelz's discovery, all of these unique cisco types had been grouped together and referred to as herring, bloater, and chubs by commercial fishing operations. They were taken at all times of the year by means of any gear possible—there was no limit. Koelz was worried that if nothing was done the unique cisco of the Great Lakes were slated for extinction.[2]

Experiencing Extinction

Extinction was not a new phenomenon in the Great Lakes region—in fact, another once abundant species had disappeared only a few years earlier. That species hadn't swum the Great Lakes; it had flown over them. Beginning around 1910, a writer named Clifton Johnson from Hadley, Massachusetts, set out on a tour of the Great Lakes, up the Erie Canal through to the Upper Peninsula of Michigan, while writing a travel book—basically a *Lonely Planet* travel guide of the early twentieth century titled *American Highways and Byways of the Great Lakes.* He captured the personal experiences of settlers he met; interviewed fishing families along the thousands of miles of shoreline he passed; rode on sailing vessels, steamers, and mule-pulled barges; and wrote about the best places to stay. As Johnson headed up the St. Clair River toward Port Huron, Michigan, he stopped at a "sleepy, decadent village" called Marysville. He tracked down "the oldest inhabitant" for an interview—an old man he didn't name who had moved to the area before the Civil War.

The man described in great detail his memories of growing up around the St. Clair River, mostly talking about one of the biggest migrations that ever occurred across the Great Lakes Basin. It was a single species, whose migration was described as a biological storm by Aldo Leopold.

"Their big flights were made early in the morning, and they went very swift," the old man recalled, "If the wind blew hard they flew high, but in a light warm south wind they flew low, just skimming along over the water or the ground or the treetops. You could throw clubs at them and get all the birds you wanted in a little while, or you could take a stout sapling with twigs on the end and whip them down. I'd go with my shotgun right over next to the woods beside a stump, and at every discharge they'd drop like hailstones."[3]

A single flock of passenger pigeons (*Ectopistes migratorius*) was estimated to consist of an average of 1.3 billion birds. Their beating wings were said to sound like stampeding horses in the sky. Passenger pigeons would take days, even weeks, to pass through midwestern towns.

The swarming behavior of passenger pigeons seems to have begun in the late 1700s, brought on by human disturbances. Historically these streamlined pigeons flourished along the entire East Coast of North America. Populations were stable for thousands of years. Heavy exploitation and habitat loss gradually pushed the species inland throughout the Industrial Revolution. Records indicate that during that time the flocks became more intense in a search for food and nesting grounds. A single breeding colony observed in Wisconsin around 1871 was recorded as 125 miles long and around 7 miles wide. "The big nesting of 1878" in Michigan was considered the last large migration ever seen. Capable of wiping out crops like a swarm of locusts, they were shot, netted, even burned in their roosts.[4]

Martha, the last passenger pigeon (named after the first First Lady, Martha Washington), died at the Cincinnati Zoo and Botanical Garden on September 1, 1914. Martha's death was the end of a species that once made up 40% of the birds of North America. John Van Oosten was 23 years old at the time; Walter Koelz was 19. The reality of the passenger pigeon's extinction was staggering. The extinction quickly became an icon for a conservation movement, drawing specific attention to our heedless exploitation of natural resources. New initiatives were taken to conserve species whose abundance was previously taken for granted, and the Great Lakes cisco fit this bill.

Saving the Cisco

At the 1927 Division of Scientific Inquiry meeting, Koelz began his opening statement by talking about the current levels of exploitation in all five Great Lakes combined: "The total annual yield of commercial fisheries has averaged around 150,000,000 pounds—of the grand total of 150,000,000 pounds, about one-half consists of species of Coregoninae, the whitefishes and lake herrings."[5] He noted that a substantial portion of the rest of that annual harvest had been lake trout. Koelz also emphasized that the annual catches had held steady all these years only because fishing pressure had constantly shifted from depleted species to other, less desirable but still marketable species.

Lake Erie had supported an annual harvest of cisco that hovered around 25,000,000 pounds, about the same weight as a group of 83 adult blue whales, for nearly a century. It was an international fishing industry. Processing and packing occurred in small towns and major cities around the lake's shared borders, and cisco were shipped all over North America and beyond. "These fish thus have sustained an almost unrestricted fishery, whose effects have been tempered only by the 'law' of supply and demand," Koelz lamented. "Fortunately, the supply has, until recently, exceeded the demand."[6] The "until recently" Koelz was referring to was the Lake Erie cisco crash of 1925.

As World War I was coming to a close in 1918, the governments of Canada and the United States implored wartime citizens to "Be Patriotic—Eat More Fish." The campaign led to steady increases fishing pressure for commercially important species in the Great Lakes.[7] In 1924 catches of whitefish and cisco were still lifted by the ton in Lake Erie. The fishery was booming. Then, in 1925, seemingly out of the blue, both species vanished to a point where only strays could be found across Lake Erie. The Bureau of Fisheries sent dozens of boats, with miles of nets, set virtually top to bottom in the lake to try and find these shoe-sized fishes with no success. The ominous disappearance sparked uproar and finger pointing within the commercial fishing and scientific communities.

As discouraging as it is that the fish are being exterminated and the waters polluted (and here I want to repeat that I am not an alarmist; the facts are plain and point to an unavoidable conclusion), it is demoralizing to realize that nothing is being done about it. No less than nine governments are administering conservation legislation, and it goes without saying that no two have the same idea! Some, in fact, have no idea at all! Control of these fisheries must be coordinated, and this clearly is possible only through a centralized body. As the waters are international, this body must be international in character. The problems that confront

The *Fulmar*, the first US Bureau of Fisheries research vessel on the Great Lakes, is under way, c. 1930s. (Photo courtesy of the John Van Oosten Library, US Geological Survey.)

other fisheries, confront the conservationist on the Great Lakes—we want to know more about the life histories of our species; we want to know whether artificial propagation does any good; we want adequate statistics; in short, we want to know everything about them, but, most of all, we want regulation of the quality and the quantity of the apparatus, or no fish will remain for us to investigate.[8]

Koelz is a pioneer in this story, but he didn't spend his career studying Great Lakes fisheries. He described eight cisco (*Coregonus*) species during his Great Lakes studies—*C. artedi* and several others, including *C. alpenae, C. hoyi, C. kiyi, C. johannae, C. nigripinnis, C. reighardi,* and *C. zenithicus*—all of which may have been unique subspecies of *C. artedi*, as hypothesized later by Reeve M. Bailey and Gerald R. Smith.[9] Of these eight unique cisco types, *C. alpenae, C. johannae,* and *C. reighardi* are now extinct and several others remain threatened.[10]

After finishing his graduate work on cisco and whitefish at the University of Michigan, Koelz became a world-renowned explorer and anthropologist. He traveled to remote areas of the American Arctic, Indian Tibet, Persia, and Nepal through the 1930s. He became best

The crew of the *Fulmar* poses for a photo while docked in Racine, Wisconsin, on August 22, 1931. *Front, left to right*, Fred A. Westerman, John Van Oosten, W. H. Muntinga, and Hilary J. Deason. (Photo courtesy of the John Van Oosten Library, US Geological Survey.)

known for his discovery of a disease-resistant wild melon in Kolkata, India, that saved a California melon crop in the 1950s. But his early Great Lakes science and pioneering advocacy for binational fisheries cooperation helped save the Great Lakes fishery. Koelz passed away in October 1989. In the years leading up to his death he donated more than 60,000 plants, birds, and fishes that he had collected from all over the world to the University of Michigan. The collection includes a few stuffed passenger pigeons and hundreds of jars of Great Lakes cisco.

Establishing Regulations

On December 5, 1928, conservation officials from Ottawa, Toronto, Illinois, Indiana, Michigan, New York, Ohio, Washington DC, and Wisconsin met for the third annual Great Lakes Fisheries Conference in

Lansing, Michigan. The primary focus of the conference for the past two years had been establishing uniform regulations and fishing gear for all jurisdictions around Lake Erie. There were no statistics or reports to show that fish stocks were collapsing. There were virtually no requirements to report catches. Van Oosten argued that quotas could not be set to protect the remaining fish populations until a way to acquire uniform fisheries statistics was developed and implemented.

The primary problem was that catch per unit of effort, a common fish population statistic, could not be calculated to determine whether stocks were collapsing or not. "We don't care about how much netting a man owns," Van Oosten stated in his first remarks at the 1928 meeting, "we want to know how much netting he is using to get the fish he is taking and how long those nets have fished to get that amount."[11] Van Oosten and others needed to know "the amount of fish taken per unit of gear, per unit of effort." At the time, commercial fishers would occasionally report how much net they had in general, even though it could be lying on docks, in storage, fishing in the water, or lying on boats. Sometimes they would report how many fish they caught, which could be over a year's time, within the last few months, or even within a day. Unless fishers reported exactly how much net they used to catch a specific number of fish within a specific time frame, the numbers reported said nothing about the status of the fish population.

Thanks to Van Oosten and others, such as D. M. McDonald, deputy minister in the Department of Game and Fisheries in Toronto, Hector H. MacKay, a biologist in the same department, Westerman, Koelz, and many more, the late 1920s gave way to a new era of fishery science for the Great Lakes—one that would be informed by population statistics. The Lake Erie fishery collapse fostered a long-lasting rapport between a binational group of Great Lakes scientists. These friendships would persist even decades later, and eventually the group would again come together. This time it would be to discuss lamprey control in the Great Lakes.

As the decline of commercial fishes continued throughout the 1930s, fishing pressure remained high. Fishing families struggled through the Depression. It was during this time, for the first time since the mid-1800s, that the catch of mainly whitefish and lake trout in the Great Lakes began to drop below 100 million pounds, roughly the weight of the RMS *Titanic*, annually. With the top of the Great Lakes food web

Lake Superior cisco are packed and stored for animal food at the Northern Cold Storage and Warehouse Company in Duluth, c. 1930s. (Photos courtesy of the John Van Oosten Library, US Geological Survey.)

removed, the base gradually became free to flourish. Populations of forage species such as smelt and alewives (*Alosa pseudoharengus*), another insidious AIS from the Atlantic Ocean that entered the Great Lakes at the same time as sea lampreys, began to expand throughout the Great Lakes. Like smelt, alewives are a little predator. Smelt and alewives formed massive schools that swept over lake trout spawning reefs. Eggs and newly hatched trout didn't stand a chance.

Commercial fishing operations were becoming more technologically advanced—it was the only way to keep up with the changing fishery. Gill nets were upgraded from traditional cotton to a more efficient nylon mesh. Boats became larger and could fish farther from port. Eventually companies built bigger, diesel-powered vessels equipped with lift arms, which began towing trawls and other actively fished nets to harvest millions of pounds of increasingly hard to find cisco. Catching cisco, smelt, and alewives became the only way to make ends meet. They began selling cisco to mink farms. The healthy oils of their meat put them in high demand by the fur industry.[12] Some unique cisco types managed to persist through the intense overharvest. The shortjaw cisco (*C. zenithicus*) was once one of the most abundant fishes throughout the deep waters (200 to 600 feet) of the upper Great Lakes—it's now one of the scarcest. Isolated populations can still be found where they were first discovered and named more than a century earlier; in Lake Superior near the "Zenith City," Duluth, Minnesota.

To make matters worse, the small-mesh gill nets, pound nets, and trap nets commonly used for catching cisco were also catching and killing substantial numbers of juvenile lake trout and whitefish. Van Oosten and Westerman found that in some areas of Lake Superior for every 150 pounds of cisco that were being caught in commercial gear 600 young lake trout were killed.[13] Commercial fishing crew members would take the small trout home to eat or market them as "mountain trout." Regulations on mesh sizes were occasionally issued yet rarely enforced due to high variability across borders.[14]

On October 12, 1931, Elmer Higgins, chief of the Division of Scientific Inquiry in the US Bureau of Fisheries, stood up in front of the Great Lakes Fishery Conference in Buffalo, New York, to talk about how wasteful the Great Lakes fishery had become. "Doubtless in overpopulated China and India no animal that comes from the waters is thrown away, but in this land of bounteous natural resources, every industry dependent

John Van Oosten (*left*) and Captain William Muntinga (*right*) of the US Bureau of Fisheries vessel *Fulmar*, seen docked at the far right, display the mouth of a deep-water trap net in Manistique, Michigan, June 12, 1932. The net has been hung by posts onshore to show its position in the water when actively fishing. This was the new technology used by the Mertz family. (Photo 1932-C-5, courtesy of the John Van Oosten Library, US Geological Survey.)

upon a natural supply of raw materials can be accused of heedless and, I may say, almost criminal waste." Higgins then pointed out that in recent years "the economic depression" had also played a role in "aggravating unfavorable conditions" for the fisheries of the Great Lakes.[15]

A year earlier, in December 1930, Van Oosten had given a similar talk to the North American Association for the Advancement of Science in Cleveland, where he discussed the results of one of his largest field studies to date related to this problem in the Great Lakes. Van Oosten's work showed that just by increasing the mesh size of trap and pound nets from two- to three-inch mesh, between 70% and 90% of undersized and nontarget fishes would be able to escape unharmed.

Higgins estimated that, based on Van Oosten's nontarget mortality study with variable mesh sizes, an additional 160 million pounds of fish were killed and dumped back into Lake Erie in the 1928 season alone.

Workers dress and salt Lake Michigan cisco for Seidl Fisheries in Marinette, Wisconsin, November 1935. A note on the back of the photo reads, "Tons are being shipped out by the barrel each week." (Photo courtesy of the Great Lakes Fishery Commission.)

The commercial fishing industry lashed back at the idea of the federal government having a say in what gear they could fish with, where, and for what. Commercial fishers reasoned that instead of regulating their equipment the government should consider stocking more fish. The uphill battle to forge international cooperation for Great Lakes fisheries management was only just beginning.

"They are fine people, but rather strange. For example, one of their strangest things is a drink called a cocktail. Here is how they make it: They put in whiskey to make it strong, then water to make it weak; gin to make it hot, and ice to make it cold; lemon to make it sour, sugar to make it sweet; then they say, 'here's to you!' and drink it themselves." Van Oosten managed to keep things light more often than not, and this was one of his jokes about how Americans are viewed by "foreigners" in his speech to the Fisherman's Club of Chicago on March 30, 1935. It was his segue into addressing the importance of international and national cooperation for the conservation of game fish. A few years earlier, at the

Group photo of the American Fisheries Society meeting in Grand Rapids, Michigan, September 2–4, 1936. (Photo courtesy of the John Van Oosten Library, US Geological Survey.)

63rd annual meeting of the American Fisheries Society, held in Columbus, Ohio, in September 1933, Seth Gordon, president of the American Game Association and secretary of the American Fisheries Society, pointed out the need for a national fish policy similar to the American game policy adopted in 1930. Both Westerman, who was president of the American Fisheries Society at the time, and Van Oosten, who was in attendance, must have listened to Gordon carefully.

As Van Oosten continued his speech, he told the fisherman's club about Seth Gordon's call for some form of "national fish policy" back in 1933 and why it was important. "As the result of Mr. Gordon's fine plea," he said, "the Council of the American Fisheries Society held a joint meeting in New York City in January, 1934, with officials of International Association of Game, Fish, and Conservation Commissioners, and agreed to sponsor an 'American Fish Policy' in cooperation with international, national, and regional groups of conservationists."[16]

Four months after Van Oosten's speech in Chicago, the American Fisheries Society appointed an International Committee of 15 members to draft an international fish policy. A tentative policy was drawn up by the committee, at which point Van Oosten noted, "Much work must still be done to put this draft in final form."[17] They didn't stop working.

Fostering Cooperation

The idea of international cooperation in managing shared natural resources was gaining popularity by the late 1930s. President Franklin D. Roosevelt visited Kingston, Ontario, and gave a speech in front of Prime Minister William L. Mackenzie King during the dedication of the international Thousand Islands Bridge on August 18, 1938. He spoke about the history of the development of the Great Lakes by Canada and United States, mentioned proposals to widen the St. Lawrence River so that "every city in the Great Lakes, now inland, would become and ocean port," and talked about the partnership between the two nations that the bridge represented.

"The development of natural resources, and the proper handling of their fruits, is a major problem of government," Roosevelt proclaimed as he discussed how the two countries hadn't always seen eye-to-eye regarding the natural resources of the Great Lakes. "Naturally, no solution would be acceptable to either country which does not leave its government entirely master in its own house. . . . In recent decades, however, we have come to realize the implications to the public—to the individual men and women, to the businessmen, big and little, and even government itself—resulting from the ownership by any group of the right to dispose of wealth which was granted to us collectively by nature herself," Roosevelt continued. But it was at the end of Roosevelt's speech that he seemed to nod toward a binational future for fisheries and water resources.

> I look forward to the day when a Canadian prime minister and an American president can meet to dedicate, not a bridge across this water, but the very water itself, to the lasting and productive use of their respective peoples. Until that day comes, and I hope it may be soon, this bridge stands as an open door. There will be no challenge at the border, and no guard to ask a countersign. Where the boundary is crossed the only word must be, "Pass, friend."[18]

On February 29, 1940, notes were exchanged between Secretary of State Cordell Hull and Canadian Minister Plenipotentiary Loring C. Christie in Washington regarding the formation of an international board of experts to "consider and recommend measures for the conservation of the Great Lakes fisheries." This was the birth of the International Board of Inquiry.[19] President Roosevelt assigned Hubert R. Gallagher and Van Oosten as the two US members. Prime Minister Mackenzie King assigned A. G. Huntsman, a pioneer Canadian oceanographer and fishery biologist, and D. J. Taylor, a government official in Ontario's Department of Game and Fisheries, as the two Canadian members.

Over the next few years Van Oosten would represent cooperative fishery management and conservation on the board, providing balance to Gallagher, assistant director of the Council of State Governments, who was chosen to maintain the interests of the states. Members of the board originally focused their attention on the urgent need to coordinate fishing legislation across state and international boundaries and to address the collapse of commercially important fishes like lake trout, cisco, and whitefish. The board felt that an international treaty in the form of a commission would be the most efficient way to address the lack of uniform regulation on the Great Lakes.[20]

The states struck back at the notion that Canada would have a hand in regulating the larger US commercial fisheries, especially with war demands placing increased pressure on fisheries' resources. The US fishing industry was three times larger than Ontario's, and the treaty would give the Canadians international regulatory power over "their fish."

An international Great Lakes fishery treaty was proposed in 1946 and quickly shot down. Predictably, the treaty was opposed because it gave regulatory power to a binational commission, taking it away from the states and provinces. With fish populations continuing to plummet, delegates immediately began drafting a new convention between Canada and the United States—completed three years later in 1949. A series of congressional hearings followed from 1949 through 1954 to work out the major kinks in the convention.

"Mr. Day, You mentioned the Great Lakes treaty through which you and Mr. Van Oosten for a period of 20 years have been trying to give away the fishing industry of the Great Lakes, the control, to the English," Congressman Alvin F. Weichel declared just moments into the start of the hearings held in Washington on March 8, 1949. "In Lake Erie about 80 percent of the fish are produced on the American side," he continued. "You know that?" "Yes, a large percentage are," replied Albert M. Day, director of the US Fish and Wildlife Service (created after the bureaus of Fisheries and Biological Survey were combined). Weichel continued, "What is the reason that you want to give to a foreign power the control of the fishing industry, especially in Lake Erie?"

Weichel, who sat on the Committee on Merchant Marine and Fisheries and was a Republican member of the US House of Representatives from Ohio, didn't see the lakes as a shared resource but rather as a property within each state. It has always been a sovereign right of the states and provinces to regulate their respective fisheries, and still is today. The state of Ohio would take a massive cut on already paper-thin profit margins of their commercial fishing industry if fishing regulations were placed in binational hands. "The English do not invite the Americans over there to control their fresh-water lakes, but you invite them over here to have something to say about ours," Weichel continued.

Day didn't back down, mainly because regulatory power was no longer proposed to be taken away from the states. "No," Day said, "This treaty is designed to do the same kind of a Job on the Great Lakes that is now done with the international commissions, the Halibut Commission and the Sockeye Salmon Commission on the West Coast, to furnish a joint means of managing the fishery that is a joint responsibility because the Canadians and the United States have joint responsibilities."

Day and Weichel continued to argue for multiple pages of transcript. Day explained that "the States would be given the opportunity to enforce the [fishing] regulations." Weichel replied, "I hope they would, on something that belongs to them. You regulate your own household; do you not?"

DAY: I try to.
WEICHEL: Then I suppose that if you cannot regulate your own yards you give it to some foreigner to handle. Do you expect to give away what belongs to the States of the Union, and give it to the English to regulate?
DAY: No.
WEICHEL: That is just what you have done in this thing in which you have urged and worked on for about 15 years, scheming against the ownership of the States. That is all.[21]

Arguments like these were common in hearings before the Committee on Merchant Marine and Fisheries, a now defunct committee of

Signing the Convention on Great Lakes Fisheries between the United States and Canada, September 10, 1954. *Front left to right,* Claude Ver Duin (US), A. L. Pritchard (Can), John R. Dymond (Can), and A. O. Blackhurst (Can); *Back, left to right,* Lester P. Voigt (US) and D. L. McKernan (US). (Photo courtesy of the Great Lakes Fishery Commission.)

the US House of Representatives, when trying to reach an agreement over who should manage the Great Lakes fishery. The solution came in a package in which regulatory power was maintained by the states and provinces while sea lamprey control was mandated by a convention between the United States and Canada. The new commission would serve a binational advisory role, manage partnerships, and act as a central hub for appropriations supporting fisheries science and sea lamprey control in the Great Lakes. A balance was struck that even the guard dogs of the states' sovereign rights, like Weichel, could get behind.

Whose Jurisdiction?

According to Dr. Marc Gaden, historian and communications director for the Great Lakes Fishery Commission, the management of the Great Lakes fishery by an international commission had been proposed more than 40 times since the beginning of the twentieth century. Through his doctoral research at the University of Michigan analyzing jurisdictional

One of the first carloads of Great Lakes cisco fillets destined for the US Army is loaded onto a railcar near Houghton, Michigan, in the fall of 1942. (Photo courtesy of the John Van Oosten Library, US Geological Survey.)

divides in Great Lakes fisheries management, he discovered that all of these proposals had failed for the same reason.

"Day viewed the issue of uniform fishing regulations *and* lamprey control as an international issue," Marc mentioned while chatting at the University of Michigan Water Center in Ann Arbor. "Weichel had every right to be worried." Marc explained that the federal government had proposed taking over regulatory authority of state's fisheries multiple times in the past; yet time after time early Great Lakes fishery treaty attempts failed because no two jurisdictions would pass the same fishing regulations. Past fisheries treaty attempts always ended with the same sentiment. "Cross-border cooperation wasn't a main priority, [while] maintaining the sovereignty of the states was," Marc said, and "the result was continued chaos."[22]

The Convention on Great Lakes Fisheries was signed in Washington, DC, on September 10, 1954. The treaty was ratified in Ottawa on October 11, 1955, at which point the Great Lakes Fishery Commission became effective.[23] For more than 60 years, the Great Lakes Fishery Commission has upheld its mandate as outlined by the convention. It works with its partners, independent commissioners, advisers representing stakeholder groups, and the agents that carry out sea lamprey control. Control agents include the US Fish and Wildlife Service, Department of Fisheries and Oceans Canada, US Army Corps of Engineers, and USGS to maintain a 90% reduction in sea lamprey populations in the Great Lakes. This comes with a price. Every year tens of millions of dollars are allocated by Canada and the United States to control sea lampreys.

That sea lamprey control would be successful was not a guarantee in the mid-1950s, as no effective sea lamprey control techniques existed. Early work in the Finger Lakes of New York had shown that a mazelike weir could help with the collection of specimens, but it couldn't eradicate or even control them. Given the grim reality that sea lampreys had become fully established in all five Great Lakes, the question on everyone's mind was how to combat a species that is fully established in an ecosystem this size and exists in several forms, including an open-lake parasitic form, a stealthy adult form that migrates in streams at night, and a larval form that lives a completely hidden life in stream muck.

CHAPTER 4

FIRST STAB AT SEA LAMPREY CONTROL

John Van Oosten sent groups out from the lab at Ann Arbor for local reconnaissance of sea lamprey spawning activity in the spring of 1938. A few spawning adult sea lampreys were observed by Dr. Hillary J. Deason, assistant to Van Oosten, in the Clinton River near Rochester, Michigan. After spending considerable time observing sea lampreys on their spawning nests, Deason suggested to Van Oosten that perhaps they could be speared, or maybe netted, at this vulnerable stage; he even suggested using a knife tied to the end of a stick as a possible option.[1]

Based on Deason's observations, Van Oosten drafted a detailed program and submitted it on May 27, 1938. The plan proposed to experiment with control techniques on the only well-known and consistent spawning river in the Great Lakes—the Ocqueoc River. Resources were spread thinner than usual at the tail end of the Depression. Plans were delayed for three more years. Conservation Officer Marvin Norton, who had conducted a personal vendetta against sea lampreys ever since he first reported them in the Ocqueoc River in the spring of 1937, took matters into his own hands while planning lagged in Ann Arbor. He began to lead excursions with members of the Presque Isle County Sportsman's Club to the falls in the Ocqueoc River, armed with pitchforks to spear sea lampreys. As spirited as these expeditions sound, it was reported that "such measures failed to halt their activities and multiplication."[2] And they probably destroyed a lot of habitat and stream banks in the process.

A vacationer filmed one of the sea lamprey spearing parties at the falls. Dr. Jim Seelye, a former supervisor in sea lamprey control, remembers the old film. It was dated 1938 with a marker and a piece of tape across the tin and was taken by a priest who vacationed in the area. Jim was interested in the film because he knew it was the earliest record of sea lampreys in northern Lake Huron.[3] Bill Swink, a retired sea lamprey biologist and a colleague of Jim's, remembers watching it when Jim copied it from a film reel to VHS tape in the 1980s. "There were definitely pictures of Ocqueoc River falls, and there were lampreys, they were out there with pitchforks, digging them out," Bill recalled. "This was 1938 or 1939 according to the license plates of the vehicles." Currently the old film is lost yet still inspiring.

Mechanical Weirs

World War II diverted resources just as a control plan was about to be initiated in 1941. In 1943 the Ann Arbor lab released a memorandum that "instructed" Michigan conservation officers to search for spawning runs. By this time, the folks in Presque Isle County were aware that spearing sea lampreys wasn't an effective means of controlling the invaders. Plans were finalized. By the early spring of 1944, construction of a control device was finally under way—an experimental weir and trap to remove the spawning sea lampreys in the Ocqueoc River.

The idea of using weirs with integrated traps for catching sea lampreys was not new in the Great Lakes Basin. As mentioned earlier in this book, in the late 1890s researchers at Cornell University were in the middle of a war on sea lampreys in Cayuga Lake, New York. An excerpt in one of H. A. Surface's manuscripts, Professor Simon Henry Gage's graduate student, stood out to me while taking another look back at this history:

> From every economical standpoint it would appear to be advantageous to rid the world entirely of the lampreys. It would certainly be greatly to the advantage of the fisheries of the State of New York if all were destroyed. Naturally, however, the student of biology must mourn the loss of a form so interesting and so instructive. The questions naturally arise: "How can the fish be protected from the lampreys; and is it possible to remove the lampreys from our lakes!"

Surface continued to explain, "Thanks to the service science has rendered by the twenty-five years' study of this subject by Dr. Wilder and Professor Gage, the *modus operandi* becomes comparatively simple." The *modus operandi* that Surface was talking about was a plan to build a weir to catch sea lampreys.[4]

Gage and Wilder recommended that sea lampreys be targeted when they are most vulnerable—during migration in shallow rivers before they have a chance to reproduce. By 1893 Gage was proposing a control program for sea lampreys in New York. He noted, "A dam with a fish-way, the fish-way leading into an isolated enclosure where the lampreys could be easily removed and disposed of, or a weir of some kind, could be constructed at slight expense." He continued, "If this could be continued for three or four years in all the lakes and in the Oswego River, the race could be extinguished and the lakes wholly freed from their devastations."[5]

The 30-plus years of work by Wilder, Gage, and Surface on the "land-locked sea lampreys of New York" finally prompted a proposal by the State Fish Commission of New York to ask the legislature for money to "totally exterminate" sea lampreys from the waters of the state. The money was appropriated through a bill signed by New York's thirty-second governor, Frank S. Black, which allocated $25,000 to be spread thinly over three years for university extension work in agriculture, which included the construction of a weir for trapping and killing spawning-run sea lampreys near Ithaca.

In 1898, a weir was constructed at the inlet of Cayuga Lake. While ultimately unsuccessful in eradicating them, the weir did reportedly catch 12,000 spawning-run sea lampreys in its first season of operation.[6] It was a primitive barrier design that funneled sea lampreys into an enclosed area to be netted by hand.[7] While it was deemed "unsuccessful" at the time, the weir designed by Gage and Surface was actually more valuable than they ever could have known, as it inspired the 1944 weir in the Ocqueoc River.

After finally receiving a plan from Ann Arbor, a Michigan conservation officer named Cyril Nelson took the lead in building the first control weir in the upper lakes in 1944. Resources were again spread thin, now more than ever during wartime. He gathered a few staff from the Department of Conservation's Field Administration and Fish Division, along with members of the Presque Isle County Sportsman's Club, and began to draft a building plan.

The weir was built just over two miles upstream from the mouth of the Ocqueoc River, just below the outlet of Ocqueoc Lake near the old CCC camp frequented by Cliff Kortman. The design was called a *conventional double-V type.* Materials for construction consisted of left-

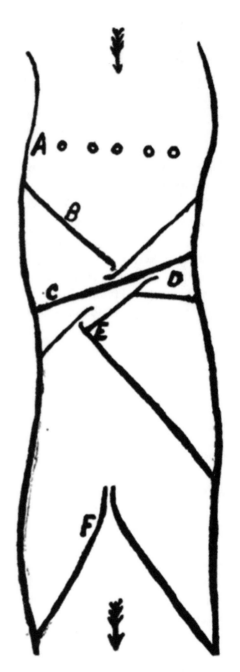

A weir design sketched by H. A. Surface, which he included on page 214 of his 1897 report "The Lampreys of Central New York." Arrows indicate flow. *A*, locations of posts to stop debris; *B*, net wings "for the capture of creatures running down the stream"; *C*, the main net stretched across the stream; *D*, a "pocket or pen" to hold the lampreys; *E* and *F*, labeled as "various wings of netting or wire."

Michigan Department of Conservation officer Cyril Nelson netting sea lampreys from the first weir in the Ocqueoc River in 1944. (Photo by James Moffett, courtesy of the Great Lakes Fishery Commission.)

over steel rock screen donated by the Michigan Limestone and Chemical Company of Rogers City and whatever old lumber they could find. While the weir installed a bit late in 1944, between May 22 and July 24 a total of 3,366 migratory sea lampreys were trapped and killed (2,000 on May 22–31, 1,225 in June, and 141 in July).[8]

The high number of catches is shocking given how faulty the weir was. I've walked this stretch of the Ocqueoc and seen the remains of this particular weir many times. The stream bed is sandy and shallow and prone to flash flooding during spring storms. David Shetter with the Michigan Department of Conservation reported that the screens would undercut, clog with debris, and blow out during high water. Sea lampreys escaped around undercut sections of each screen. Other fishes, such as common suckers, would get trapped and take hours to separate from the sea lampreys. Any by-catch would need to be removed by hand and moved upstream. It was by all accounts a brutal first season.

Mechanical weirs continued to be modified over the next several

Amiable Robbie Thompson of Sturgeon Bay holds three sea lampreys caught in the Department of Lands and Forests weir on the Sturgeon River, a tributary to Lake Huron near Simcoe County, Ontario, May 1, 1957. (Photo published in the *Midland Free Press*, used with permission from the Huronia Museum of Midland, Ontario.)

years in an attempt to make them more effective. The Ocqueoc River weir was rebuilt in 1945 and was up and running before the sea lampreys entered the river, this time catching more than 4,500. The Michigan Department of Conservation reported the results of the Ocqueoc season to Wisconsin, and in the spring of 1945, an Ocqueoc-inspired weir was installed in Hibbard's Creek on the Door Peninsula by the Wisconsin Department of Conservation. The weir in Hibbard's would be operated by Matt Patterson for the next four years.

By 1946 Ontario's Department of Lands and Forests was beginning to experiment with weirs and traps, mainly around northern Lake Huron in the North Channel and around Georgian Bay. Ontario went one step further and tested hoop nets, which that they referred to as "lamprey nets," traditional cotton-mesh nets with a structure consisting of a series of steel hoops. These nets were clumsy and heavy and commonly wiped out during spring floods.

Meanwhile, sea lampreys were continuing to devastate the fishery. George Purvis, president of the Purvis Brothers Fishery on Manitoulin Island, Ontario, comes from a long line of commercial fishers. His family's roots fishing Georgian Bay and northern Lake Huron reach all the way back to 1882. "The first sea lamprey that they saw here, apparently, they say they brought it to shore in 1934," George said as we sat in his net shed in 2017. "They played with it and thought, 'This is a real oddity'."

The Purvis family's fishing business was at the epicenter of sea lamprey destruction—directly across Lake Huron from the Mertz fishery. "The fish were dead on the bottom of the lake, especially in the fall when they were spawning," George told me. "If you swept your nets a bit on the bottom and pulled them up, the tugs would stink so bad you couldn't stand to be on the boat." George explained that members of the crew would have to wear something over their faces when around the dead fish, most of which bore lamprey wounds. I was surprised to learn that after most of the larger lake trout were gone, the sea lampreys quickly switched to smaller fish, mainly whitefish. "We would get a washtub full of lamprey every day attached to the whitefish," George said. "It didn't take long [for the sea lampreys] to decimate a population, and they did it in about ten years." Looking back in George's extensive catch records while sitting in his office, it did look bad. A note there read, "In 1947, we didn't have one lake trout."

Ontario conservation officials constructed two rigid Ocqueoc-

Purvis Brothers Fishery workers lifting a pound net off Burnt Island, Ontario, in northern Lake Huron, c. 1940. (Photo courtesy George Purvis.)

inspired weirs in the Little Thessalon River, and caught more than 11,000 sea lampreys in 1946—more than double the total number taken in the Ocqueoc River weir in the previous two seasons combined. None of the other five net designs caught more than 100 lampreys per net. The officials decided wire-mesh Ocqueoc-type weirs would be the only ones used in the following years.

Electrofishing

The largest sea lamprey spawning runs were occurring throughout tributaries to northern Lakes Huron and Michigan and southern Lake Superior by the 1950s, and the earliest control attempts were focused on these regions. In 1945 the Wisconsin Department of Conservation began experimenting with early electrofishing gear that would shock the larval sea lampreys out of the mud so they could be caught. As you can imagine, early attempts at mixing electricity and water were dangerous and ineffective.

John Van Oosten noted that in an early field test "considerable time" was needed in the field to catch about 250 larvae in Hibbard's Creek.[9] The first electrofishing units had a gas-powered generator that sat on shore and two electrode paddles on wooden poles that were tethered to the generator, which could be used by two individuals to shock larvae

Emmet Peterson (*left*) and Don Allen (*right*) of the early sea lamprey control crew in Ludington, Michigan, show off the new and improved backpack electrofishing gear that Don pioneered c. 1965. Since Emmet had a physical disability, missing half of his right arm, which prevented him from holding both electrode paddles, Don developed an electrode that attached to Emmet's boot so he could fish with one hand. (Photo courtesy of the Great Lakes Fishery Commission.)

out of the muck in one small area of the river. The generator would have to be inched by hand along the muddy banks as the biologists continued sampling. Far worse was the fact that no emergency shutoff switch existed if a worker fell in.

Eventually the units were reduced to a backpack style that one individual could wear, making the biologist look like a Ghostbuster. Bill Greene remembers the old back-mounted fish shockers well. He grew up in Sault Ste. Marie, Ontario, and around 1956 he would regularly see control biologists surveying streams for sea lampreys near his home just outside of town. "I knew the office was on East Street over top of what used to be the post office at that time. It's now the museum," Bill laughed as we sat in the new offices of the Fisheries and Oceans Canada Sea Lamprey Control Centre (SLCC) just up the road on Queen Street. "They had their office upstairs, so I went up there and talked to them, had an interview," Bill said. "Then they hired me." Bill worked in sea lamprey control for the next 46 years.

One of his first tasks in the late 1950s was checking old mechanical weirs similar to the one used in the Ocqueoc River. These weirs were scattered along tributaries north of the Soo in the Ontario waters of Lake Superior. He also spent his first months surveying those same streams for larval sea lampreys. "I think the voltage was with a DC voltage, about 150 volts, and that depended on the water and the distance between the electrode paddles," Bill said as we talked about how terrible it was lugging the backpack shockers through thick brush.

The units were powered with an old lead-acid motorcycle battery. "Yeah, you could always tell the person that did the shocking," Bill laughed. He explained that if you tipped or leaned over while working in the scum-covered rocky rivers, the batteries would leak and burn holes in your clothes. "They did not have a mercury switch," Bill added, an automatic shutoff switch developed later that would cut the electricity if you fell. "You just hoped you didn't touch the electrode when you went down."

From these early adult-trapping and larvae-shocking attempts, it was quickly realized that more money and research were needed if control of sea lampreys was to be achieved. Federal action for sea lamprey control originated at the municipality level throughout coastal towns around Lakes Michigan and Huron—sea lamprey hot spots. Resolutions were adopted by several cities and counties, including Alpena, Rogers City, Frankfort, Manistique, Schoolcraft County, and Gladstone, all in Michigan; Manitowoc and Milwaukee, Wisconsin; and Waukegan, Illinois.

On June 12 and 13, 1946, the Subcommittee on Fisheries of the Committee on the Merchant Marine and Fisheries of the House of Representatives held a hearing in Washington, DC. The top of the hearing transcripts, in bold, capitalized text, reads "MENACE OF THE SEA LAMPREY." Statements were given by Claude Ver Duin, president of the Michigan Fish Producers Association and creator/editor of the popular Great Lakes commercial fishing publication *The Fisherman* from Grand Haven, Michigan, as well as Van Oosten, Deason, and William Flory, who was acting director of the Fish and Wildlife branch of the US State Department. Also submitted was a July 1937 article from *Michigan Conservation* titled "Spread of the Sea Lamprey through the Great Lakes."

"As Dr. Van Oosten has indicated, I believe the problem must be tackled in every area in which spawning runs do exist, so that in addition to initiating control operations in areas where there are established runs, we must push our search for additional runs and institute control measures," advised Hilary Deason as he spoke to Congressman Fredrick Van Ness Bradley regarding Van Oosten's work with the sea lamprey invasion over the past few years. He added, "It will be an expensive program, I am sure."[10]

Congressman Bradley, a Republican from Rogers City, Michigan, was more than willing to submit Van Oosten and Deason's sea lamprey control program as a joint resolution. He told Deason, "If you will get that up to me and submit it to me, I will say this, that I am going up to Michigan at the end of this week, and I will be up on Lake Huron, Lake Michigan, and Lake Superior next week, and I will make some more first-hand inquiries among the fishermen, and I will be glad to introduce the legislation."

The sea lamprey problem was in Congressman Bradley's backyard—this AIS impacted people he knew personally. He introduced H. J. Res. 366, the first congressional bill requesting appropriations for sea lamprey control, a day into the hearings. It was titled "Joint resolution authorizing and directing the directory of the Fish and Wildlife Service of the Department of the Interior to investigate and eradicate the predatory sea lampreys of the Great Lakes." Without Bradley's tremendous legislative action and support, history may have been written very differently in the Great Lakes. Just one year later Bradley passed away at the age of 49—abruptly ending his time as chairman of the Committee on Merchant Marine and Fisheries in the 80th Congress.

Unlike the past several decades of fishery management disagreements over the Great Lakes, no one flinched at the idea that cooperation and federal aid from the US government were needed to combat sea lampreys. Resolutions identical to Bradley's were later introduced by Republican congressman Alvin Weichel of Ohio (H. J. 367) and Republican senator Homer Ferguson of Michigan (S. J. Res. 168). Weichel and Ferguson were both alums of University of Michigan, and perhaps it was their shared alma mater that forged such wonderful cooperation on the sea lamprey issue. Or perhaps it was the fact that destruction by this AIS was in everyone's backyard: the Great Lakes, the heart of North America. If something wasn't done about the sea lampreys soon, there would be no more fish in the Great Lakes to argue over.

The committee amended H. J. Res. 366 and submitted it to the House on July 10, 1946, and it passed only nineteen days later, on July 29, by unanimous consent. President Harry Truman signed the resolution just a few days later on August 8. While Res. 366 allocated to the Fish and Wildlife Service the humble sum of $20,000 annually for ten years to "investigate and eradicate" sea lampreys, Congress lagged on actually appropriating the funds. The clock kept ticking, and Michigan got tired of waiting.

The Fish and Wildlife Service tried to set up a cooperative program with various US states and Ontario, but the state of Michigan was the only one to cooperate at the time. The Michigan state legislature appropriated $40,000 to be spent over four years to research control methods for sea lampreys. The funds went through the Michigan Department of Conservation to be made available to its research section, the Michigan Institute for Fisheries Research. Congress finally came through with its appropriation toward the end of 1946. Taken together, enough resources were secured to begin assembling a research team.

By now the Michigan Department of Conservation and the Fish and Wildlife Service had built a long-lasting rapport, forged on the slimy backs of sea lampreys. Yet the program needed cooperation from all eight US states bordering the lakes and Ontario if the program was going to work. After all of the political hype during the summer of 1946 settled, Van Oosten began to plan the first binational sea lamprey control committee for the Great Lakes. His first step was to reflect on the damage already done by sea lampreys. Throughout Lakes Michigan, Huron, and Ontario, commercial fishers were reporting from 25% to 80% of the lake trout damaged by sea lampreys. He reflected on what was known about the sea lampreys' life cycle, where potential weak spots might be, and what still needed to be discovered. Early researchers, such as Coventry and Dymond at the University of Toronto and Wilder, Gage, and Surface at Cornell University, had pieced together some of the details regarding the basic life history of sea lampreys more than 60 years ago, and Van Oosten cited their work regularly in his notes.

Van Oosten's plan was to arrange an informal meeting with conservation officials from mainly Wisconsin (Dr. Edward Schneberger, superintendent, Fish Management Division, Wisconsin Department of Conservation, Madison), Michigan (Fred A. Westerman, director, Fish Division, Michigan Department of Conservation, Lansing), and Ontario (Hector H. MacKay, supervisor, Game-Fish and Hatcheries, Fish and Wildlife Division, Department of Lands and Forests, Toronto) to convince them to participate in an annual Great Lakes sea lamprey conference. All four had a rich history, having worked on Lake Erie fishery issues together more than 20 years before.

Bob Braem (*right*), a pioneering sea lamprey control biologist who worked from 1950 to 1983, sits with a crew in northern Michigan during an early sea lamprey spawning stream survey, c. 1950. (Photo courtesy of the Great Lakes Fishery Commission.)

A logical choice for Van Oosten's informal meeting was to piggyback it with an American Fisheries Society meeting to be held on September 11–13, 1946, in St. Paul, Minnesota. Van Oosten's meeting was held one day in advance, on September 10. I picture the meeting taking place in a smoky hotel lounge, with whiskey. Whether whiskey played a role in the closed-door meeting or not, Van Oosten's efforts paid off. He called for a "master plan" to "avoid duplication," and "assure comparability of results" for sea lamprey work around the Great Lakes. He wanted to have regular conferences on sea lamprey control, and he noted that this was to "check progress of work and workability of methods." The officials from Michigan, Wisconsin, and Ontario agreed, and no time was wasted planning the first official meeting.[11]

Great Lakes Sea Lamprey Committee

The first official conference of the aptly named Great Lakes Sea Lamprey Committee (GLSLC) was held in Ann Arbor on November 14–15, 1946. In Van Oosten's opening remarks, he related a sobering truth about past coordination attempts.

This is the first international conference of Great Lakes fisheries representatives ever held at Ann Arbor in spite of the fact that this city has been the headquarters of the principal researches conducted on the commercial fisheries of these lakes. This conference has been called primarily to integrate the various programs of control of the sea lamprey and thus to avoid unnecessary duplication of effort among the states, the Province of Ontario, and the U.S. Federal Government.[12]

Word of the first sea lamprey conference traveled fast. More potential partners began to contact Van Oosten, specifically from New York, Pennsylvania, and Ohio. Conservation officials from fisheries departments in Wisconsin, Michigan, Ontario, Ohio, New York, Pennsylvania, Indiana, Minnesota, and Illinois and various commercial fishermen from throughout the Great Lakes Basin were also present at the first GLSLC meeting. The goal was to share knowledge on what had been done, and agree on what still needed to be known, in the looming battle against sea lampreys.

Ontario, Michigan, and Wisconsin had the most to offer in terms of preliminary investigations, and the sea lamprey infestation was still primarily focused in their waters. Each had already built various weirs, experimented with larval-sampling methods, and surveyed commercial fisheries. Van Oosten lamented the failed attempts and lessons learned thus far: "Digging larvae out of the mud with a dip net is ineffective and too expensive, so also is killing of adults on nests with knife, spear, gaff hook, or other hand equipment, or catching them by hand or with dip net or seine; so also is destroying nests."

The main control techniques were still focused on destroying spawning-run adults. Van Oosten proposed a "two-way weir, similar to the one operated by Ontario in Killarney," which were "successful in stopping migrating adults" during the 1946 season. Next he proposed constructing experimental traps to suit various types of streams. Knowing that each stream is a unique system, he proposed that the committee consult regularly with net manufacturers and commercial fishers—the ultimate catchers of fishes. Other ideas were thrown about.

- Make sure someone followed up on a mysterious device built to kill sea lampreys at a dam on the Manistique River, a tributary of Lake Michigan in Michigan's Upper Peninsula. Although there are no photos, this device sounds like it is straight out of medieval times. Workers from the power plant noticed sea lampreys had been attaching themselves to the face of the dam. They placed a sheet of metal in the river, positioned like a ramp, which allowed water to flow down it. Sea lampreys would work their way up the flowing metal ramp until they dropped over the edge to their deaths "in a bucket of oil."

• Look into importing American eels, natural predators of sea lampreys on the East Coast, to stock them in Lake Superior as a biological control option.

• Consult others to develop methods to capture parasites in the open lake.

• Consult companies about placing electric screens or similar devices at mouths of rivers.

• Develop a portable and more efficient electrical shocker for sampling larvae.

• Determine the effect of electrical currents on larvae and eggs.

• Develop dredges or other devices to capture larvae.

The GLSLC understood that, while killing adults would rid the system of one generation, killing larvae would remove upward of five to seven generations at once. The problem was physically getting at the larvae. Copper sulfate, a common fish poison, was suggested as "a means of destroying the larvae in streams" in 1946 but not taken seriously. The committee noted that coal mine pollution was often tolerated by lampreys, and that "before chemicals affect the lampreys, one-half of the other fish species may also be affected."[13] Still, the idea of chemical control would linger as a footnote for the next several years—never fully disappearing from the mix of ideas.

Many questions still remained at the end of the meeting.

• Do sea lampreys at any stage have natural predators?

• Why do some sea lampreys choose certain streams over others?

• What types of substrates do larvae prefer?

• Can larvae be located and destroyed by some rapid method?

• Can age groups of sea lampreys be determined from length and weight data?

• Why do they metamorphose?

Bob Braem stands on a walkway board leading from the bank to a trap in the Little River, Oconto, Wisconsin, c. 1950s. Hans Bowers and Wes Ebel are emptying the trap. (Photo courtesy of the Great Lakes Fishery Commission.)

- Do some stay in inland lakes accessible from the Great Lakes?
- Finally, how do we get the public more involved in supporting sea lamprey control?

Commercial fishermen commonly attended meetings to offer advice. The majority felt the time had come to stop the sea lampreys. Oliver H. Smith, a multigenerational commercial fisherman out of Port Washington, Wisconsin, acted as a regular adviser at early sea lamprey meetings. "From the time the warning was sent out by Dr. Van Oosten in 1927 or 1930, there has been a great increase of sea lampreys seen," he said before the GLSLC in 1946. "At one time, ten percent of the fish caught had been attacked; now it is fifty to seventy-five percent—fishermen are looking for some way to combat this menace."[14]

Oliver Smith, as well as many others, had good reason to volunteer for things like manning weirs or reporting scars. Smith Bros. Fisheries, which was established in 1848, was just beginning to go out of business by 1946 due to the sharp decline of lake trout and whitefish in Lake Michigan. Like everyone, Smith was motivated to save his business. Over the next decade he would keep his business afloat mainly by redirecting his effort toward harvesting and marketing whitefish and cisco. He was an advocate for conservation of the fishery, a hard worker, and a firm believer that one of the worst things ever to happen to the Great Lakes fishery was the invasion of the sea lamprey.

Claud Ver Duin was present at the 1946 GLSC meeting, and one of his stories in his opening remarks struck me. Ver Duin mentioned that a fisherman he knew over in Lake Huron had recently set 14 boxes of nets on one of the best trout reefs in the lake for 5 days, an abnormally long time to let ones' nets stay in the water, and didn't catch a single trout. Ver Duin, who would later become one of the first commissioners of the Great Lakes Fishery Commission, knew that this same amount of net and effort back in 1940 would have produced 12,000 pounds of lake trout in Lake Huron. Instead, the fisherman he was talking about caught 300 pounds of badly scarred burbot (*Lota lota*).[15]

It should be noted that burbot, historically considered to be nonmarketable, and therefore a "trash fish," were often killed and thrown back for no reason. Burbot are a native Great Lakes predator and ecologically important species in the lakes for thousands of years. They're also a freshwater relative to the marine cod, and they taste great.

The sea lamprey was fully blamed for the perils of the fishery by 1946, but even back then there were some who knew this disaster wasn't wholly the sea lampreys' fault. Outdoor writer Johnny Mock published an article in the July 23, 1946, edition of the *Pittsburgh Press* headlined "Nets, Not Eels, Deplete Trout: Commercial Fishers Raise Familiar Cry." In his narrative, Mock said flat out that commercial fishermen are always looking for someone else, or something else, to blame for the depletion of commercial fishes. But "One fault with many of the commercial fishermen has been they will take the very last fish from a certain section and then move to another location to repeat the performance."[16]

Mock was skeptical of the variation in scarring reported throughout the lakes at this time. In northern Lakes Huron and Michigan, as well as most of Lake Ontario, fish were looking like they had been held to a belt sander. Yet even in these heavily infested waters there was still a lot of variation in scarring. As an example, the Wisconsin Department of Conservation sent out a detailed questionnaire in 1946 to commer-

Sea Lampreys attached to a burbot. (Photo courtesy of the Great Lakes Fishery Commission.)

cial fishing operations in Lake Michigan, mainly around Green Bay. The form was circulated by Matt Patterson, who wanted to get estimates of sea lamprey scarring. Of 300 surveys sent out, 92 came back. Of the 170,000 pounds of lake trout caught, approximately 40% were described as scarred by sea lampreys. Only 15% of those scarred lake trout were actually refused for sale, yet roughly 34% were discounted because of the scars. These are the same waters where up to 80% scarring had been reported in other surveys.

Patterson was frustrated with the low number of responders to the questionnaire. From March 3 to April 2, 1947, he made personal trips on commercial fishing vessels to observe the lake trout for himself and determine whether or not scarring was a real problem. From his observations mostly around Racine, Kenosha, Milwaukee, Port Washington, and Sheboygan, all in Wisconsin, he recorded that of the 902 lake trout he examined, 216 (23%) were what he called "badly scarred," while 191 (22%) had one fairly unnoticeable scar and the remaining 495 (55%) were untouched by the parasites. He reported that the opinions of the fishermen at the time were also at both ends of the spectrum: some were very worried that scars would impact prices while others didn't seem to care in the least.

The variation in sea lamprey damage in different regions of the lakes was eventually linked to varying degrees of suitable spawning habitat, pollution, and suitable prey. If Mock were still around, I'm sure he would be interested to know that nets and sea lampreys, as well as pollution, recreational fishing pressure, habitat loss, and introduced species, all "depleted trout."

In Canada commercial fishermen had also been working closely with the Ontario Department of Lands and Forests (ODLF), the predecessor of the Ontario Ministry of Natural Resources (OMNR), on the sea lamprey problem. Things were escalating in Georgian Bay and near the North Channel. Carl F. Kolbe, a multigenerational fisher and director of the Ontario Commercial Fishermen's Association in Port Dover, reported at the 1946 GLSLC meeting that there wasn't much commercial fishing for lake trout in Lake Huron throughout Ontario waters "because sea lampreys and fish declines were so bad." He warned that "not one trout is caught in gill nets without lamprey marks." Like many commercial fishers in the highly infested regions of the Great Lakes, Kolbe was growing impatient with the amount of research that was being proposed. He made a point of emphasizing that fishermen around the lakes "will not be wholly satisfied to see the attack made on lampreys only in an experimental way for the next five years." Yet Kolbe understood that things could not be done overnight. "The fishermen will have to learn to take the lamprey out themselves," he declared in his final remarks.[17]

Lamprey on the Menu

As is human nature, one of the first questions everyone asked in the early days of sea lamprey control was whether these newcomers could be marketed. Dr. Peter Tack, of the Michigan State College's Zoology Department, attended early GLSLC meetings for this reason. Dr. Tack recently began conducting studies on "utilization of the less popular fishes." He suggested that the experts involved in these studies would be willing to take sea lampreys, experiment with cooking and preparing them, and look into publishing recipes that would be made available to the public.

Unfortunately, sea lamprey flesh is a grayish color and, in my opinion after dissecting thousands of them, smells like a mixture of fish, mud, and melted plastic. In the Great Lakes, sea lampreys accumulate heavy metals and toxins in their flesh after feeding on multiple large-bodied fishes that themselves have accumulated these pollutants, which continue to circulate though the food web after hundreds of years of industrial abuse.

The idea of marketing sea lampreys for consumption is nothing new. As mentioned earlier, lampreys have long been a delicacy in Europe, and the custom was brought to the East Coast of North America. In writing this book, I couldn't stop thinking about what a bad idea it is to attempt to eat sea lampreys. According to the twelfth-century English historian Henry of Huntington, King Henry I, son of William the Conqueror, died after eating too many of these creatures against the advice of his physician. Perhaps this was from simply gorging himself on them to a deadly extent during one of his trips to Normandy. Either way the toxic qualities of this animal's tissues were *roughly* understood since the king's death on December 1, 1135. It's still not clear whether lampreys are actually toxic or just accumulate toxins from their hosts.

Vernon Applegate made dozens of attempts to make sea lampreys palatable. His notes about these experiments start off grim: "Preliminary experiments indicated that spawning run sea lampreys were quite unpalatable." In 1947 he caught 12 sea lampreys in a weir constructed in Carp Creek, now called the Black Mallard River, which still flows just a few miles up the road from the Ocqueoc River. He took his catch to a smokehouse owned by Mr. Emil Plath of Rogers City. Mr. Plath had smoked meat and fish commercially for more than 35 years at this point and was a leading smoked meat authority in the area. Applegate noted that Plath was "particularly interested in determining if the lampreys would make a saleable smoked product."

The results were what you would expect. The smoked lamprey flesh was noted to be "streaked with black from the original blue discoloration of the flesh," which Applegate referred to as "accumulated waste products." In his notes, he wrote, "The appearance was unappetizing and texture of the flesh was soft or mushy." He went on, "The most unfortunate characteristic was an acrid, unpleasant odor, characteristic of the lampreys but unlike the usual 'fishy' smell of other fishes." What Applegate was seeing was the bioaccumulation of heavy metals and other toxins.[18]

After three separate failed attempts to cook sea lampreys for friends, Applegate finally came to his conclusion: "The slimy skin, the snake-like appearance, and the ugly mouth and head brought forth expressions from outright disgust to a complete disinterest in experimenting with

Cranbrook Institute of Science director Dr. Robert T. Hatt takes a shot at cooking a sea lamprey in June 1953. (Photo courtesy of the Great Lakes Fishery Commission.)

them as food." A few failed attempts by Applegate weren't going to stop others from trying. "After preparation, we passed [sea lamprey] samples around to some unsuspecting friends who found them very tasty and appetizing" Van Oosten wrote in a letter in 1949.

Van Oosten regularly spoke about the false ideology of "eradicating" sea lampreys from the Great Lakes. "Newspapers sometimes give the

Vernon C. Applegate lifts a small gill net with a few tangled spawning-run sea lampreys in the mesh while conducting graduate work in Ocqueoc Lake on June 25, 1947.
The fact that he was able to catch any sea lampreys in a net like this, and in a lake
connected to the river, shows the magnitude of the infestation at the time. (Photo
courtesy of the Great Lakes Fishery Commission.)

impression that this committee expects to eradicate the sea lamprey
in the Great Lakes, and some report that in cannot be done," he said,
"The problem is one of control—you cannot expect the sea lamprey to
be eradicated any more than you can expect to eradicate all undesirable
insects, rodents, and predators." The GLSLC agreed with Van Oosten
that the notion was a pipe dream. "Some practical method of holding
down the numbers of these parasites is the goal toward which all of our

activities should be pointed," Dr. Gerald P. Cooper decreed in an update for Michigan. "I suspect that the lamprey will be with us like fleas on a dog from now on."[19]

Cooper was a staff member of the Michigan Institute for Fisheries Research at the time, a cooperative research unit between the University of Michigan and the Michigan Department of Conservation. Aside from his interest in working out which specific actions the states should undertake and which duties the US Fish and Wildlife Service should assume, Cooper was the connection behind establishing a lamprey control base at the old CCC camp on the Ocqueoc River. He informed the committee that the camp had been turned over to the Parks Division of the Department of Conservation. This was a prime location for early sea lamprey research on the shores of Ocqueoc Lake, just footsteps away from the heavily infested Ocqueoc River. There was plenty of room to initiate experiments on sea lampreys.

Coordinating Efforts

With the missing links outlined and a research headquarters confirmed at the former CCC camp on Ocqueoc Lake, all that was needed was a graduate student to take on the work. Vernon Applegate was identified by Karl Lagler, an assistant professor in the Department of Zoology at the University of Michigan and the Institute of Fisheries Research, a cooperative program between the university and the Michigan Department of Conservation, as a top candidate for the sea lamprey study. Applegate received his undergraduate degree (1943) and master's degree (1947) at the University of Michigan. He had been working with Lagler since 1943 on projects ranging from length-weight relationships in snapping turtles to "observations on the primeness of a fall collection of muskrat pelts."[20] After serving for a year in World War II, the 28-year-old Applegate was awarded a research fellowship with the Michigan Institute of Fisheries Research once congressional and state funds were secured for 1947.

Although he was based in Ann Arbor, Applegate spent his graduate research seasons at the CCC camp up north from 1947 to 1949—work that would eventually result in his PhD dissertation, the *Art of War* for battling Great Lakes sea lampreys, "Natural History of the Sea Lamprey, *Petromyzon marinus*, in Michigan."

In four years, Applegate was able to complete his doctoral research

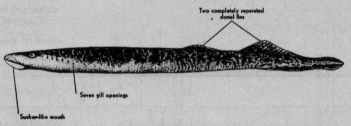

FISHERMEN!
YOUR COOPERATION IS REQUESTED

THE SEA LAMPREY IS SPREADING RAPIDLY THROUGH MICHIGAN WATERS AND IS BELIEVED TO BE A MENACE TO THE COMMERCIAL FISHERIES OF OUR STATE. THE DE-PARTMENT OF CONSERVATION IS ENGAGED IN A PROGRAM TO LEARN METHODS OF CONTROL OF THIS FISH PARASITE.

SEA LAMPREYS MIGRATE INTO MANY OF OUR STREAMS AND RIVERS EACH SPRING TO SPAWN.

IF YOU SEE ONE OR MANY OF THESE PARASITES IN A STREAM OR RIVER, PLEASE NOTIFY THE LOCAL CONSERVATION OFFICER OR THE NEAREST STATE FISH HATCHERY. OR, IF THIS IS NOT PRACTICABLE, WRITE CONSERVATION DEPARTMENT, LANSING.

Two completely separated dorsal fins

Seven gill openings

Sucker-like mouth

SEA LAMPREY

Adult sea lampreys usually will be more than a foot long. They usually appear mottled with brown and black on the backs and they may have a somewhat golden tint.

MICHIGAN DEPARTMENT OF CONSERVATION

The sign Applegate posted around Michigan in 1947 and 1948 requesting the aid of the public in reporting sea lamprey spawning runs. (Reprinted from Applegate, "Natural History of the Sea Lamprey in Michigan," 9.)

and produce substantial data regarding the general ecology and physiology of sea lampreys in the Great Lakes, including (1) distributions of spawning runs, (2) the relative abundance of sea lampreys, (3) sex ratios of spawning runs, (4) length-weight relationships, (5) migratory habits, (6) pathology and diseases that may infect lampreys, (7) reproductive potential, (8) spawning habits and behavior, (9) physiology of adults and larvae, (10) economic studies regarding damage caused by sea lampreys, and much more. He didn't do it alone. Robert Frank and Floyd Simonis, both of the Michigan Department of Conservation's Fish Division, were just a few of the individuals that assisted Applegate during most of the research. Perhaps the most important of all these discoveries were details about the larval life cycle gleaned through the use of a new type of barrier, which Applegate called an "inclined screen trap."

The new screen trap was actually the idea of Mr. Philip Wolf of Malmoe, Sweden.[21] The trap was designed to filter an entire river for lampreys. Everyone wanted to know how long they remain larvae before transforming into adults. It all began with Applegate's "chute-and-barrel-type" trap constructed at the Carp Lake river outlet near Mackinaw City, Michigan, in 1948. The trap was a rough first draft, designed to catch downstream-moving, or newly transformed, sea lampreys before they could enter the lake. After tweaking the design in 1949, the weir was modified into what was called a "dam and inclined screen trap." The trap functioned like an industrial-sized colander in which everything upstream of the dam was caught on a screen as it came down, including newly transformed sea lampreys; yet nothing could get back upstream past the dam. The inclined screen trap at the Carp River outlet would eventually lead to the monumental discovery that sea lampreys can remain in larval form in the sediment for more than 7 years, in some cases up to 17. Newly transformed sea lampreys were still being caught in the screen more than a decade later as they drifted down from the headwaters above the dam. Applegate had the mysteries of the larval sea lampreys, and general life history of the adults, solved by 1949.[22]

With the ecology and life history of the Great Lakes sea lamprey understood, it was time to focus on methods to control them. What the GLSLC needed now were field technicians and biologists to assist Applegate with field-testing new types weirs and traps. Field crews were needed to travel around the Great Lakes and look for new sea lamprey populations. More scientists were needed to research new control techniques.

The year 1949 brought with it a turnover of directors in the GLSLC. Van Oosten resigned as chair and director of the Great Lakes fishery lab in Ann Arbor in 1949, and Dr. James Moffett was nominated to replace him. Moffett ushered in a new era, concluding that the time for life history investigations was past and that of the application of control devices had arrived. To Moffett the sea lamprey problem was now "an operational procedure." Although Congress would appropriate more funds toward the end of 1949, Moffett emphasized that such funds were becoming more difficult to secure. He suspected that there was a feeling among members of Congress that the states should devote more of their own funds to the problem.[23]

Still commercial fishers and fisheries scientists throughout the basin continued to lobby for federal assistance. Congress appropriated funds for sea lamprey control toward the end of 1949, a $250,000 federal appropriation to be added to an annual $10,000 from Michigan, catalyzing a rapid expansion of the program. The new appropriation recharged the pursuit of a new and effective way to control sea lampreys. It also allowed dozens of new hires in 1949—among which stood Cliff Kortman. The crew rapidly outgrew the small barracks of the former CCC camp.

Early sea lamprey control biologists rigging supports for an electrical barrier c. late 1950s. (Photo courtesy of the Great Lakes Fishery Commission.)

A direct current (DC) guidance barrier and trap (*far left*) in the Chocolay River, a tributary of southern Lake Superior in Michigan, in 1958. (Photo courtesy of the Great Lakes Fishery Commission.)

Sea lamprey control biologists check a mechanical spawning weir and trap in the Root River, a tributary of Lake Huron in Ontario, in June 1956. (Photo courtesy of the Sea Lamprey Control Centre and Great Lakes Fishery Commission.)

Vernon Applegate's inclined screen trap used to capture recently transformed parasitic sea lampreys at the Carp Lake outlet, in Michigan, in July 1958. Downstream-moving sea lampreys would drop over the dam and onto a screen, seen toward the right of the photo with a broom and shovel on top. (Photo courtesy of the Great Lakes Fishery Commission.)

Recently transformed sea lampreys captured in river nets during the 1970s. (Photo courtesy of the Great Lakes Fishery Commission.)

Early tests on selective toxicants in the HBBS raceways, c. late 1950s. Holding cages containing experimental groups of larvae can be seen toward the center of the photo. (Photo courtesy of the Great Lakes Fishery Commission.)

An HBBS biologist applies TFM at an application feeder site during one of the first Lake Superior tributary treatments, c. late 1950s. (Photo courtesy of the Great Lakes Fishery Commission.)

One of the first remote chemical analysis trucks with equipment used to analyze treatment concentrations in water samples during the first treatment of the Pays Plat River, northern Lake Superior, Ontario, in the fall of 1959. (Photo courtesy of the Sea Lamprey Control Centre and Great Lakes Fishery Commission.)

Jack Miron (*left*) and J. J. Tibbles (*right*) motor along the Pays Plat River looking for spots to treat with lampricide during the fall of 1959. (Photo courtesy of the Sea Lamprey Control Centre and Great Lakes Fishery Commission.)

Sea lamprey control in tributaries of Lake Superior began before major roads were built (e.g., the Trans-Canada Highway 17). Early sea lamprey control crews often paved their own way to get to remote locations for treatments. Here an Ontario control crew crosses the Old Woman River outside Wawa, Ontario, in July 1960. (Photo courtesy of the Sea Lamprey Control Centre and Great Lakes Fishery Commission.)

Frank Green, Shelly Zettler, and Don Holmberg fix a broken generator during a remote Lake Superior treatment in 1961. (Photo courtesy of the Sea Lamprey Control Centre and Great Lakes Fishery Commission.)

Dead alewives form a windrow in Chicago Harbor in Lake Michigan, c. mid-1960s. (Photo courtesy of the John Van Oosten Library, US Geological Survey.)

City officials spray dead alewives on a Chicago beach with disinfectant, c. mid-1960s. (Photo courtesy of the John Van Oosten Library, US Geological Survey.)

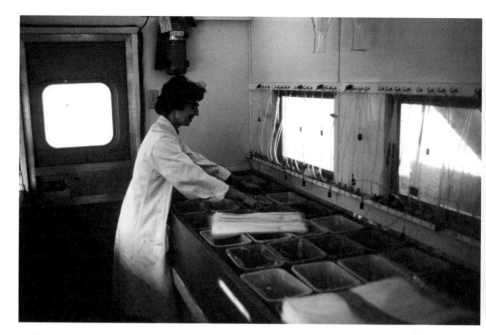

H. Elizabeth (Liz) Cormack, a student assistant with the Fisheries Research Board of Canada, London, Ontario, Biological Station and Technological Unit, prepares to conduct lampricide bioassays in a trailer for remote Lake Superior treatments in 1961. (Photo courtesy of the Sea Lamprey Control Centre and Great Lakes Fishery Commission.)

B. G. Herbert Johnson, a pioneering sea lamprey control biologist, analyzes water samples for TFM concentrations during a treatment in 1962. (Photo courtesy of the Sea Lamprey Control Centre and Great Lakes Fishery Commission.)

A helicopter delivers TFM and supplies at a remote campsite near the mouth of the Pic River, northern Lake Superior, Ontario, in 1963. (Photo courtesy of the Sea Lamprey Control Centre and Great Lakes Fishery Commission.)

A sea lamprey control crew conducts an early treatment in the White River, Lake Superior, Ontario using granular Bayer 73 and TFM, in 1963. It still wasn't known at this point if the lake trout of Lake Superior could be saved from the sea lamprey infestation. (Photo courtesy of the Sea Lamprey Control Centre and Great Lakes Fishery Commission.)

A sea lamprey control biologist with the hose used to administer lampricides. The perforated hose typically lies submerged across the stream during treatment. (Photo courtesy of the Great Lakes Fishery Commission.)

Doug Cuddy conducts a fluorescein dye study in preparation for a TFM treatment in Lindsey Creek, a tributary of Lake Ontario in New York, in 1976. (Photo courtesy of the Sea Lamprey Control Centre and Great Lakes Fishery Commission.)

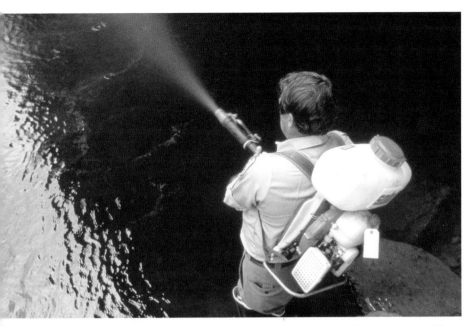

A Solo blower used to apply granular Bayer 73 during treatments, c. 1980s. (Photo courtesy of the Great Lakes Fishery Commission.)

A homemade pontoon craft used to spray granular Bayer 73 during an August 1967 treatment of the Thessalon River in northern Lake Huron, Ontario. (Photo courtesy of the Sea Lamprey Control Centre and Great Lakes Fishery Commission.)

Control biologists collect spawning sea lampreys from their nests by hand at the Quance Dam on Big Creek in eastern Lake Erie, Ontario, in 1981. (Photo courtesy of the Sea Lamprey Control Centre and Great Lakes Fishery Commission.)

Lee Hanson of the HBBS crew takes notes during one of his pioneering male sea lamprey sterilization studies near Tahquamenon Falls, Michigan, in June 1988. (Photo courtesy of the Great Lakes Fishery Commission.)

A portable trap full of spawning-ready sea lampreys is lifted using a small crane from the St. Marys River in Sault Ste. Marie, Ontario, in 1991. (Photo courtesy Sea Lamprey Control Centre and Great Lakes Fishery Commission.)

A sea lamprey control team from the SLCC in Sault Ste. Marie, Ontario, marks adult sea lampreys with fin clips for later population estimation studies in 1987. (Photo courtesy of the Sea Lamprey Control Centre and Great Lakes Fishery Commission.)

Sea lamprey control crews from Canada and the United States work together to treat an infested section of the St. Marys River's Little Rapids cut, September 1988. (Photo courtesy of the Sea Lamprey Control Centre and Great Lakes Fishery Commission.)

Don Dubin (*left*) and friends with a fine catch of Lake Michigan chinook salmon, c. 1980s. (Photo courtesy Don Dubin.)

A rainbow trout jumps over a low-head V-shaped weir and sea lamprey trap in Stokely Creek, a tributary of Lake Superior, Ontario, in 1981. (Photo courtesy of the Sea Lamprey Control Centre and Great Lakes Fishery Commission.)

Control biologists from Canada and the United States can be seen standing in boats searching for dead and dying larval sea lampreys after the St. Marys River Little Rapids lampricide treatment, September 1988. (Photo courtesy of the Great Lakes Fishery Commission.)

A sea lamprey control biologist treats the Manistique River, Michigan, c. 2015. (Photo courtesy of Ted Lawrence, Great Lakes Fishery Commission.)

Sea lamprey control biologists conduct secondary lampricide treatments in backwater areas of Bear Creek, Michigan. (Photo courtesy of Ted Lawrence, Great Lakes Fishery Commission.)

CHAPTER 5

DISCOVERING A CHEMICAL ASSASSIN

As you head west from Rogers City on the coastal highway US23, you pass miles of sandy Lake Huron beaches. Dense forests pass by to your left. On a sunny day, Lake Huron's shades of deep green fade into robin's egg blue before hitting shore—the view rivals the best days on the Caribbean. At a small dust-blown turnoff called Ray Rd., down a steep hill, and around a corner there is a currently bustling biological station that sits on a point overlooking Hammond Bay. The first thing you'll notice is the 1 million gallon water tank built a few years ago that provides head-pressure to irrigate tanks and raceways throughout the entire facility. Yet, at the center of all of the new buildings sits the original, the nearly 150-year-old, US Life Saving Service boathouse—complete with hand-carved beams, white paint, and a red roof.

The lifesaving station was built in 1876, served for more than 70 years as one of 54 lifesaving stations on the Great Lakes, and was decommissioned in the late 1940s. The station had been vacant for a few years before Applegate made the suggestion to Moffett in 1949 that this would be an ideal location for a new lamprey control base. Moffett agreed. The US Fish and Wildlife Service, using the recent appropriation from Congress, secured the facility from the Coast Guard and hung a new hand-painted sign above the door: Hammond Bay Fishery Laboratory. The station would change names multiple times throughout the next 60 year, but never break its focus on developing new sea lamprey control methods. Currently the sign out front reads US Geological Survey—Great Lakes Science Center Hammond Bay Biological Station, in partnership with the Great Lakes Fishery Commission (HBBS).

Cliff Kortman had worked in sea lamprey control for about six months by the time the new station was established in 1950. He moved to HBBS as part a new permanent staff of 17 individuals, with an equiv-

The Hammond Bay Biological Station as it looked when it was converted from a US Life-Saving Service station, c. 1950. (Photo courtesy of the Great Lakes Fishery Commission.)

alent number of summer employees. Cliff told me that the place was in pretty rough shape when they first moved in, but it could have been worse. A caretaker had frequented the property for a few years after the buildings were abandoned. There was one phone, no water, and eight old buildings surrounding the original boathouse. As I chatted with Cliff, he mentioned that HBBS almost looked like a forgotten village when he checked the place out for the first time.

Applegate was selected as head of the station, and Cliff was in charge of handyman work—carpentry, plumbing, and building/checking sea lamprey weirs. With the help of Cliff, HBBS was immediately retrofitted with running water, tanks, net shops, boathouses, and office spaces. Cliff would also conduct routine sea lamprey work with the crew. "Every morning we would have to go and empty the traps," he told me. He weighed and measured the sea lampreys they would catch each day during the run and bring them back to the lab to dispose of them. Sometimes he would handle more than 500 sea lampreys in one day, scooping them out of the traps by hand and wrestling them into an old metal cream can so they could be run back to the station for experiments.

LIFE CYCLE OF THE SEA LAMPREY

Cliff Kortman, an avid artist, was the first to draw the life cycle of the sea lamprey in the early 1950s. Here he shows his novel work in his home in Rogers City, Michigan. (Photo by the author.)

Cliff worked on the weirs until about 1954. He left to serve in the Korean War as a cook based in Austria and came back to northern Michigan in 1956. "And then, when I come back," he chuckled, "I went down the next day and Applegate said, 'You're coming to work.' I said, 'No I'm not, I want to stay home a day,' so the next day I went back to work." There was something new and urgent going on at the station.

"Moffett said we had to come up with a chemical that would kill the sea lamprey without harming the fish," Cliff told me as he showed me his old laboratory at HBBS. "Dr. Applegate said 'Well, why don't you weigh the chemical' and then I started weighing the chemical." Cliff had weighed his share of sea lampreys, could build a weir or even a building, but he never thought he would do anything like this. With no background in chemistry, he jumped right in to lead the chemical bioassays. He would weigh all the chemicals for the next 31 years.

In all, Cliff weighed more than 7,000 types of compounds by hand with an old triple-beam balance under a fume hood in a corner of the station. This was the golden age of the "pickle-jar biologist," as the five-gallon glass pickle jar was the original standard vessel used to run acute toxicity tests in fisheries science.[1] A few trout and larval sea lampreys were thrown into a series of jars, different concentrations of a chemical were added to each, and researchers waited to see what died first. Cliff became so accurate that he could weigh out as little as 0.005 grams, which he explained was about the weight of the amount of graphite it takes to sign your name in pencil.

At this point in talking with Cliff I began to wonder why everyone at HBBS had become so focused on finding a selective toxicant to kill sea lampreys. I remembered the old meeting minutes and the fact that the idea of chemical control had barely rated a footnote in the late 1940s meetings. What had happened that caused everyone to revisit the possibility of controlling sea lampreys in just a few years?

John Van Oosten had tossed around the idea of poisoning sea lampreys in the past, but it was almost always dismissed because everything in the stream would need to die before all the larvae could be effectively killed. The complexity of the poisoning method was made clear when a study was conducted in 1948 using a common fish poison called rotenone in an attempt to kill larval sea lampreys.

Albert Hazzard of the University of Michigan's Institute for Fisheries Research in Ann Arbor reported on a preliminary poisoning study that turned into a mess: "Experiments with an organic poison, rotenone, for killing the larvae while in the stream were entirely negative," he reported. The details of the test weren't given, but you can assume that whatever stream was chosen for the test was wiped clean of any aquatic life for a spell. He went on to report, "Poisoning of spawning populations has not been attempted and is not recommended as it would be necessary to render a stream lethal to all fish life for a four month period at the expense of the spawning activities of many food and game fishes."[2]

Cliff Kortman at his HBBS bench in the mid-1950s weighing chemicals for bioassays. (Photo courtesy Cliff Kortman.)

Rotenone, extracted from the roots of a species of plant (*Derris ellip-tica*) found throughout Southeast Asia, has long been used as an insecti-cide and fish poison. At one point, the odorless and colorless compound was considered to be a selective toxicant for fish, but the selectivity was based on physical, not physiological, modes of action. In 1941 John Greenbank of the Michigan Department of Conservation published "Selective Poisoning of Fish" in the *Transactions of the American Fish-eries Society* after he discovered that he could poison warm water fishes without harming cold water trout in the same lake.[3] This was because the poison didn't mix with the deeper cold waters where the trout occurred. Greenbank was inspired to develop the poisoning method based on work that had been done in 1938 in Fish Lake, Utah, under the direction of Stillman Write. Write was able to poison entire spawning shoals of a "destructive chub" because of the way the fish accumulated in the shallows during its reproductive season. This was also a physical, not physiological, selective poisoning. Although it was never proven, it had been suspected since the 1930s that rotenone often left nontarget "food organisms" alive after a poisoning compared to the more traditional copper sulfate fish poison.[4] Moffett was familiar with the past work of Greenbank, as both had worked together at the Institute for Fisheries Research in the late 1930s—Moffett as an aquatic biologist and Green-bank as a research assistant.

Despite a few failed poisoning attempts, immediately after he became chair of the GLSLC in 1949 Moffett began redirecting research efforts toward selective toxicants. In his first report as chair, he noted that con-trol efforts should be directed toward development and testing of "phys-ical or chemical means." He was referring to the poisoning of both adults and larvae. He mentioned the use of "barrier dams, ultrasonic vibra-tions, and possibly repellent chemicals" to stop spawning-run adults and "chemical destruction of larvae" to wipe out multiple generations in streams at once. At the 1949 meeting, Moffett stated that a primary goal would be to test "various chemicals in attempt to find substance of maximum specific toxicity to ammocoetes [pronounced "ammo-seats"] but doing minimum of injury to fish or substance with short-term toxic action."[5] They would also test "methods of application of chemicals."[6]

Moffett's charge to discover a chemical killer specific to sea lampreys occurred during a boom of pesticide development and use—a progres-sive era in chemistry and scientific exploration combined. The produc-

Left, Philip J. Sawyer (photo courtesy of the Milne Special Collections and Archives Department, University of New Hampshire Library, Durham, New Hampshire); *right, top*, Sawyer conducts the first "pickle jar" bioassays to find a selective toxicant for sea lampreys while being filmed by Vernon Applegate (photo courtesy of the Great Lakes Fishery Commission); *right, bottom*, Sawyer's test setup (photo by Philip J. Sawyer, courtesy of the Great Lakes Fishery Commission.)

tion of pesticides, mainly herbicides and insecticides, spiked after World War II. Total pesticide production in the United States jumped from less than 100 million pounds in 1945 to more than 300 million pounds by 1950. Between 1947 and 1952 alone, the US Department of Agriculture registered nearly 10,000 new pesticides. These were mainly for the control of nuisance insects and weeds.[7]

The roaring pesticide movement of the 1950s, coupled with the growing development of rotenone and copper sulfate fish-poising programs, inspired Moffett to reignite the idea of the first selective lamprey poison. In 1949 Moffett immediately began to request money for another graduate student to investigate selective toxicants for sea lampreys that wouldn't harm other fishes.

One of the new faces that showed up when Cliff and the crew moved to the new HBBS facility in 1950 was that of Philip J. Sawyer—the new selective toxicant graduate student. Sawyer was awarded a fellowship at

University of Michigan through the Fish and Wildlife Service. Given that a lowly graduate student was never invited to attend meetings among fisheries professionals, Applegate described Sawyer's main task to the committee as "conducting an exhaustive search for a specific toxicant which will kill larval lampreys while in their burrows." Within a few months of beginning his work at HBBS, Sawyer had completed 121 tests on 42 different compounds, and his results were already looking positive. "The great majority of these compounds kill larval lampreys in concentrations varying from 0.125 ppm[parts per million] to 5000 ppm. If, and when, promising toxic substances are found, they will be applied and tested under stream conditions by permanent staff personnel," Applegate reported to the GLSLC at its annual meeting in 1950. He added, "Some solution to the problem of distribution of the toxins will also be considered."[8]

By 1951 Sawyer had made some progress in identifying chemicals that would kill larvae yet leave other fishes alive, but the results were spotty. In his update at the 1951 GLSLC meeting, Applegate mainly talked about barriers, but he included a note about Sawyer's work: "Continuation of a research fellowship provided by the Service permitted a doctoral candidate in the University of Michigan to extend a comprehensive search for a specific toxicant which will kill larval lampreys while in their burrows." By this point, Sawyer had conducted more than 530 tests on 179 compounds. Most of these chemicals killed more fish than lamprey larvae, and an equal number killed both the larvae and the fish. "A few compounds, 14 to be exact, have shown varying degrees of specificity in killing larvae," Applegate stated. "One of these compounds, a restricted chemical, has shown great promise. At concentrations of 1 ppm to 5 ppm its toxic effects on larval lampreys are more pronounced and more rapid than on other test species." Applegate concluded, "Further investigation of this compound is currently underway."[9]

Back at HBBS, Sawyer had been experiencing considerable difficulty in obtaining sufficient chemicals to test. Applegate assisted Sawyer by reaching out to the National Research Council, which eventually sent 208 additional compounds to HBBS while simultaneously placing the station on a list to receive new chemicals in monthly shipments. By the end of 1951, Sawyer had several compounds that were selectively toxic to larval sea lampreys at various efficiencies.

Applegate didn't hold his breath that a selective toxicant would solve the sea lamprey problem at this point. He made it clear that his main goal in 1952 was to develop an electrified screen that would stretch across a river and create an electrical field to guide migrating adults into traps, or otherwise kill them. It was a dangerous contraption called an electric weir. Funds to keep the research going at HBBS were too unpredictable to start another project like chemical screening, and he knew that the development of electrical weirs had already accounted for a major portion of research money.

Still, Sawyer continued with hundreds of compounds using typical "pickle-jar" bioassays, placing a few larval sea lampreys and a few trout in a jar, adding a chemical, and seeing what dies first. Sawyer found that six compounds were selectively and consistently killing larval sea lampreys. He checked these six chemicals for similarities and found that all six had nitro groups. More specifically, all six could react with water to form a nitrophenol.[10] Sawyer didn't know it at the time, but his research would pave the way for the discovery of one special mononitrophenol that would conquer the Great Lakes sea lamprey. He wouldn't remain at HBBS to see it happen.

Sawyer's doctoral research on selective toxicants, and his time at HBBS, came to an end by 1952, at which point he had collected enough data in three years to begin writing his dissertation, published in 1957. On December 16, 1952, at the Hotel Savery in Des Moines, Iowa, Applegate gave a brief statement to the effect that Sawyer's search for a selective toxicant had been "terminated during 1952," referring to the completion of his graduate work. Applegate went on to state that Sawyer's work "has been a laboratory screening study of chemicals, made in an attempt to find a substance highly toxic to larval lampreys in concentrations harmless to fish." Applegate mentioned that several promising compounds had been discovered through Sawyer's bioassays, "but field tests will be required to determine their practical value."[11]

Sawyer was drawn back to his alma mater, the University of New Hampshire, where he would continue to write his dissertation while simultaneously transitioning to a new teaching position. He went on to have an incredible career at the university until his retirement in 1982. He taught topics in zoology and aquaculture and even formed his own aquaculture company. Sawyer passed away in 2001. He is known for his career in aquaculture, as a natural teacher who knew and loved the outdoors, and is renowned for his discovery of the first selective toxicants effective against sea lampreys.

Electrical barriers like this one on the Brule River in northern Wisconsin, c. 1950s, were an early attempt to block spawning runs of invasive sea lampreys in the Great Lakes. While they could stop migrating sea lampreys with their electrical current, these barriers killed other fish and animals that got too close and were sometimes nicknamed "death fences." (Photo courtesy of the Great Lakes Fishery Commission.)

Applegate was eager to discuss electric weirs at the 1952 meeting. "The entire effort during the coming spring [of 1953] will be directed at completing the installation of the control devices [electric weirs] in the pilot control program for Lake Superior." Applegate was focused on the urgency of saving the last of the lake trout remaining in Lake Superior, and electric weirs were thought to be the sea lamprey's silver bullet.

But the focus of research at HBBS didn't shift entirely toward development of electric weirs. In 1953 the HBBS crew began screening 50 chemicals a day under a directive given by Moffett. Moffett made sure the chemical screening continued, and was excited by Sawyer's findings.

"The situation points to the urgency for extension of control to all Unites States streams of Lake Superior and for intensive research on possible methods of destroying ammocoetes in larval beds," Moffett declared in a 1953 annual report. The situation that Moffett was addressing was the rapid expansion of sea lampreys into Lake Superior. "Regardless of measures taken, a severe decline of the Lake Superior lake trout fishery seems probable."[12] Moffett kept the research focused on killing larvae and discovering the first ever physiologically selective chemical assassin of an aquatic vertebrate.

Applegate's electrical weir research, while still under way, was quickly dismissed as a complete solution for the sea lamprey problem toward the end of 1953. It wasn't because the devices weren't working; it was because Applegate wasn't sure HBBS, or any sea lamprey control program for that matter, was going to exist for much longer. In his quarterly report to Dr. Ralph Hile, assistant chief to Moffett at the Great Lakes Fishery Investigations lab in Ann Arbor on August 28, 1953, Applegate began by writing, "I am afraid that the following is the best statement I can make of our rather confused activities during the past 90 days." Applegate explained to Hile that all his experimental electrical weirs were being pulled out of the rivers in anticipation of complete loss of funding. "As a result of a threatened drastic curtailment of funds, most of the months of June and July were dissipated in removing field installations from streams and storing such equipment on the Hammond Bay Fishery Laboratory grounds; further effort was expended in preparing the laboratory for being closed for an indefinite period."[13]

But an appropriation of funds did come through in 1953. With the new money, all experimentation with electrical weirs and all "construction and operation activities" of these weirs were transferred to a new facility in Marquette, Michigan. Back at HBBS, the focus remained to continue as a center for research in developing new sea lamprey control techniques. The laboratory was converted to a facility for screening what Applegate estimated would be about 6,000 compounds in a search for a chemical which would be non-toxic to other stream organisms, yet still kill sea lampreys. This shakeup at HBBS marked the beginning of the chemical bioassay years.

By December 1953 Applegate and the crew at HBBS began screening compounds at their full capacity. Applegate reported to Moffett on December 17, "As of today we are operating the 3 troughs which can be used to full capacity—39 tests simultaneously. We managed this by instituting a laboratory work procedure which resembles a Notre Dame backfield play—with flourishes . . . it all hinges on using every available minute for weighing chemicals." Applegate didn't have the resources or equipment to operate chemical bioassays at this capacity; rather he was referring to the cumbersome job of weighing exact amounts of each compound and the fact that it was *fumbling* the entire operation. Applegate's crew were derailed with failing pumps, breakdowns, and inadequate laboratory equipment. "I sure hope we will be able to borrow a better laboratory scale," he notes toward the end of his letter.[14]

The new search for a selective toxicant created a problem immediately. The station needed more compounds to test. Sawyer's work suggested that some kind of nitrophenol might hold the key to selectively killing larval sea lampreys, but these chemicals were rare. A small vial of these types of compounds may have been collecting dust in a university laboratory here and there, but that was about it. Applegate began contacting companies and universities around the nation to ask for a sample of their chemicals.

Records of the types and amounts of chemicals that began pouring into the station were loosely kept, if at all, in the 1950s. Tracking down this information is a nearly impossible task, but Rosalie "Roz" Schnick did it. Roz worked as a research librarian with the US Fish and Wildlife Service's National Fishery Research Lab in La Crosse, Wisconsin, now the USGS Upper Midwest Environmental Science Center (UMESC). Roz began to piece together the origins of chemicals tested at the station for a pivotal review paper she published in 1972.[15] Without the research that Roz conducted throughout the 1970s, most of the history behind the early sea lamprey chemical bioassays would have been lost.

Roz found that HBBS had around 4,000 compounds shipped to them that had already been tested for toxicity in other fishes (not sea lampreys) under the direction of Robert E. Lennon at the Fish and Wildlife Service's US Fisheries Station at Leetown, West Virginia, which is currently the USGS's Leetown Science Center National Fish Health Research Laboratory. The lab in Leetown subjected several species of fishes to these compounds in pickle jar bioassays and categorized the chemicals into three groups: (1) very toxic, (2) moderately toxic, and (3) negative.[16] From there the compounds were labeled and shipped to HBBS. So many compounds arrived from Lennon at the Leetown lab that HBBS couldn't keep enough bioassay record cards (data sheets) on hand, in which case someone had to travel to Ann Arbor, nearly 240 miles away, to print more on what they commonly referred to in letters as "the Zoology Department's ditto machine."

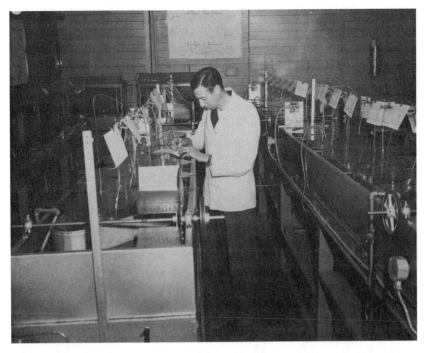

Conducting chemical screening bioassays to find selective sea lamprey toxicants at HBBS, c. 1950s. (Photo courtesy of the Great Lakes Fishery Commission.)

Within a year, workers at HBBS quickly found themselves with more compounds on hand than could be handled. In addition to the 4,000 compounds that would come from the Leetown lab, HBBS received more than 2,000 compounds from all over the world—from private companies, dynamite manufacturers, chemical companies, paper companies, universities, basically any organization that used chemicals.[17]

The fate of HBBS in 1955 was again uncertain. Funding wasn't guaranteed for the coming fiscal year. On January 29, 1954, Applegate and Moffett had a long discussion in Ann Arbor about "the desirability of accelerating our chemical screening program and the possibility of accomplishing this 'speed-up' by operating on a seven-day-a-week basis." They came to an agreement to optimize the time they had, concluding, "The greater number of compounds tested, the greater our chances will be of discovering a specific larvicide."[18]

Personally I'm amazed by how urgent and complicated the search was at this point—and that no one was giving up. By February 1954, the Hammond Bay crew had conducted 1,250 tests on 1,133 chemical compounds in its "search for a specific larvicide." Applegate wrote to Dr. Ralph Hile of the Fish and Wildlife Service in Ann Arbor that, "Although several compounds have been found which kill larvae at concentrations of 5 ppm, these substances also killed trout and bluegills which were also used in the tests." He concluded, "No specific larvicide has been discovered to date."

In 1954 and 1955, HBBS focused almost exclusively on finding a selective toxicant to kill sea lampreys. Morale at the station stayed high. The bioassays constantly tormented Applegate and the crew with results that looked promising at first and then proved to be entirely negative. According to Applegate's notes, by 1955 eight compounds were determined to be selectively toxic to sea lamprey larva, with two considered especially promising. The two compounds had codes: no. 174 and no. 3579. Compound no. 174 (3-bromo-4-nitrophenol) came from Lennon's lab in Leetown. The other, no. 3579, was described as O-ethyl-S-pentachlorophenyl thiocarbonate. Both compounds would kill larval lampreys at only 1 to 3 ppm without "typically" harming other fish in the laboratory tests.[19]

Applegate passed away in 1980, but historian Tom Kutchenberg conducted what was likely the last interview with him in 1978. Tom reached Applegate by phone and asked him what it was like to lay eyes on the first promising compound after thousands of failed tests. Applegate, who was known to speak his mind, replied:

> The fellow who was working with me came upstairs and said, "You better come down here and take a look at something that is happening in one of the test jars." I looked and said, "What the hell chemical is that?" because they were all code numbered. We went into the records and found the name of it and we thought, "It must be a mistake. We'll run it again." We ran it and re-ran it and kept getting the same results.[20]

The compound Applegate was talking about was 3-bromo-4-nitrophenol (no. 174)—a cousin compound of the group found by Phillip Sawyer a few years before. But there were problems. Both 174 and 3579 were rare, complicated to produce, and had been difficult to dissolve in water during artificial laboratory experiments.[21] Compound 3579 worked best when water temperatures were very cold, just above freezing, but began to kill everything when temperatures warmed. Additionally, the only way to get 3579 to dissolve in water was by first dissolving it in acetone, which couldn't be applied in the field.

Back in 1955, a pound of custom synthesized 3-bromo-4-nitrophenol cost about $1,600, approximately half the starting annual salary of a biologist at the time. Making matters worse, neither compound could be produced in a pure form. Each batch contained contaminants that ruined the selectivity of the chemicals. Both compounds were dropped from the running toward the end of 1955, and the focus shifted to other chemicals, both inside and outside the nitrophenol family.[22]

The station sent out another solicitation for chemicals. By this time, Applegate had refined his list of questions that needed answering.

- Was there a similar chemical that could be found that was more economical to produce at a sufficient purity to maintain its action as a selective poison?
- If a new chemical existed, could it be concentrated enough to be schlepped into the woods and the upper tributaries of Great Lakes streams for application?
- Would the new chemical dissolve properly in a solvent that could be applied? If so, would the solvent itself influence the activity of the chemical?
- Could a pump be built that would administer the chemical in a sufficiently uniform and consistent way to maintain a specific lethal concentration in a stream for a set amount of time?
- If a new chemical was found, would a company be willing to continuously produce it for a steady sea lamprey control program?
- Would any of these chemicals actually work outside the laboratory?

HBBS was now a well-oiled machine for chemical testing with a crew that had the determination and pioneering spirit to keep everything running. Tests were conducted like clockwork. A constant supply of larval lamprey and finger-sized rainbow trout was kept at the facility. Up to 100 bioassays were being run simultaneously each day. Tests were in water that was kept at exactly 55°F. Each morning the results were recorded; dishware emptied, cleaned, and refilled with fish and larvae; chemicals weighed; and new tests begun. The experiments ran 24 hours a day, day after day, for the next two years.

The crew had determined that the toxic selectivity of certain compounds to larval sea lampreys was more specific than Sawyer or anyone else had imagined, unique to a group of mononitrophenols containing halogens. Candidates were narrowed down from about 40 compounds to roughly a dozen. The compound had to be a mononitrophenol. In other words, it had to have one nitrogen group on its benzene ring, the aromatic ring that makes up the body of the compound. If two nitrogen groups were on the ring (dinitrophenol) you could have either a general pesticide that kills everything or a controversial weight loss drug known as DNP that was banned in the 1930s. Just like any drug, even a small modification in molecular structure could have dire consequences for field testing.

The experiment couldn't have been any closer to the wire. Sea lampreys had fully infested the basin at this point and had even spread into some of the inland lakes of the region. The fate of the remaining Great Lakes lake trout looked grim. The commercial fishery, once the heart of the Great Lakes economy, was on the beach, and invasive alewives and smelt were beginning to show signs of a population explosion.

The continued requests for mononitrophenols yielded another six promising chemicals in 1956. John Howell and Vernon Applegate applied for a patent for no. 174 in case it might still be usable in the future. Dr. Clarence L. Moyle of the Dow Chemical Company had been coordinating a chemical supply to HBBS and suggested around nine compounds similar to no. 174. One of these compounds, 3,4,6-trichloro-2-nitrophenol, later nicknamed "Dowlap," was promising in laboratory tests at HBBS, making it an ideal candidate to test in the field. Dow was capable of producing a large batch of Dowlap. While laboratory tests were promising, everyone at HBBS knew from the beginning that an actual field test would be the moment of truth. In the face of uncertainty, no time was wasted in getting enough Dowlap synthesized for a test in a wild stream.

Cliff came back from the Korean War and was handed official chemical-weighing duties by Applegate on the brink of moving selective toxicant studies into the field. But years of false alarms had hardened Applegate; he and his research partner, John Howell, kept laboratory bioassays going at full capacity with little expectation that Dowlap would work. Applegate's optimism was wavering after what amounted to 15,000 *mostly* failed bioassays testing 5,000 compounds.

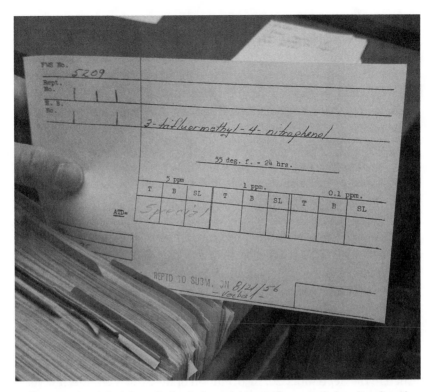

Cliff Kortman's original data slip for the lampricide 3-trifluoromethyl-4-nitrophenol
(TFM) sees the light of day for the first time in more than 60 years as we searched
through towers of old HBBS files. (Photo by the author.)

Cliff continued running bioassays with the rest of the HBBS crew
day and night. "That's what we did every hour on the hour," Cliff told me.
"We'd set it up at about maybe ten o'clock, Clyde would always wash the
dishes, Howard and Ben were there to help tear it down," he explained.
Cliff made sure to tell me that it was a tremendous team effort.

Then Cliff told me about a day that will forever be remembered in
this story. On August 21, 1956, as Cliff arrived at the station and made his
way into the laboratory to check the bioassays, he saw exactly why Moffett, Applegate, Lennon, Hile, Howell, and others had been so excited
over the past few years. Sixty years later, Cliff still correctly told me that
this was the 5,209th chemical he had weighed at HBBS. There in front of
Cliff, in the jars, the larvae were stiff, pale, dead. The small lake trout and
bluegills were darting back and forth, very much alive.

"I couldn't believe it," said Cliff, lighting up as if the discovery had happened yesterday. After running tens of thousands of failed tests with thousands of strange compounds, the sight was enough to cause Cliff to simply write the word *special* where data were usually entered on the test card and immediately head upstairs to Applegate's office to deliver the news in person. "Nobody ever thought that it could be done, that you could find a chemical that kills a certain vertebrate without killing something else," Cliff said with a big grin. The scientific breakthrough that Cliff saw that day was caused by a yellowish powder, a mononitrophenol known as 3-trifluoromethyl-4-nitrophenol, TFM for short, another cousin compound to Dowlap.

Something was indeed *special* about this particular mononitrophenol. It worked extremely well, better than all of the other compounds identified so far.[23] But Dowlap had already been chosen for the first field tests and was currently in mass-production at Dow Chemical. The money had been spent. For now TFM would be put on the back burner, though not forgotten.

News of plans for the first field test began to buzz through the media. In the fall of 1956, reporter Lloyd Lockhart of the *Toronto Star* visited HBBS to interview Vern Applegate about the research for a story published in the September 29, 1956, edition of the *Star Weekly*. A few years later, in 1958, Lockhart would be the last man to interview Ernest Hemingway while roaming around Cuba for the *Star*. It seems Lockhart had a knack for being where big stories were happening.

"At 34, this could be his hour of triumph," Lockhart wrote about Applegate and his pending field test. He described Applegate as "a slight, sandy-haired graduate of the University of Michigan" and began the interview by asking him what his expectations were of actually finding a selective chemical killer. "I've worked with lampreys so long no matter what happens now it's an anti-climax," Applegate replied, "Sometime soon I'd like to go after another menace—the carp." Applegate continued to digress to common carp (*Cyprinus carpio*) control. "Our government spent $500,000" trying to bring carp under control last year with methods that weren't effective, Applegate said. "The carp is just as undesirable as the lamprey. Maybe a special chemical is needed there, too."

Even with a bit of pessimism on Applegate's part, Lockhart noted that the scientist "shuddered to think what will happen if chemicals fail to stem the lamprey depredations." In the interview, Applegate explained that electrical weirs had done a fine job killing adults, but they weren't accounting for "the six generations of lampreys [in streams as larvae] waiting to burst forth as killers. We cannot afford to waste a moment at present," he concluded.[24]

By April 1957, about 10 mononitrophenols had been singled out as effective at different levels. Dowlap was selected for the first field test. The top ten compounds were now as follows.

- 2-bromo-4-nitrophenol
- 3-bromo-4-nitrophenol (no. 174)
- 2-chloro-4-nitrophenol
- 5-chloro-2-nitrophenol
- 3-fluoro-4-nitrophenol
- 2,5-dichloro-4-nitrophenol
- 3,4,6-trichloro-2-nitrophenol (Dowlap)
- 3-trifluormethyl-2-nitrophenol
- 2-trifluormethyl-4-nitrophenol
- 3-trifluormethyl-4-nitrophenol (TFM, aka Lamprecid 2770)

Before any field tests were completed, Applegate and Howell applied for a US patent for the control of sea lampreys with mononitrophenols. They applied for a Canadian patent for the same compounds later in March.

News of the success of artificial laboratory raceway tests at HBBS using Dowlap had reached the *Milwaukee Journal* after updates concerning the experiment were given at a commercial fishing advisory meeting in Wisconsin in late July 1957. The experiment was unlike anything the public had ever heard of, seeming more like a blind and desperate shot in the dark than an actual experimental investigation. A typical headline was "Chemical Way to Kill Sea Lamprey Found: Dowlap Raises Hopes for Revival of Lake Trout Fisheries in the Great Lakes."

Laboratory tests looked good, patents were filed, but one more task remained: The chemical needed to be proven safe for other creatures before the researchers would allow Dowlap application in the field. Additional subjects included in the laboratory raceway tests were brook trout, brown trout, bullheads, various caddis fly larvae, central mudminnows, common shiners, various crayfish, creek chubs, lake chubs,

Cliff Kortman shows off a dead larval sea lamprey killed in the first lampricide field test in Little Billie's Creek, Millersburg, Michigan, October 29, 1957. (Photo courtesy of Cliff Kortman.)

logperch, longnose dace, mottled sculpin, rainbow trout, rock bass, sunfish, various turtles, white suckers, and yellow perch. The lab tests used water from local streams, as well as rocks, sediments, and even aquatic weeds. Larval lampreys were consistently and selectively killed across all tests. Lloyd Lockhart asked Applegate if he was worried that larval sea lampreys would become immune to a selective toxicant like this during his interview. "Immunity comes from survivors," Applegate replied. "We have never had any survivors."[25]

It was the moment of truth. On October 29, 1957, in Little Billie's Creek (now Elliot Creek), a small sandy creek that meanders through mostly private forest and empties into Hammond Bay just up the road from HBBS, the crew began to set up for a very big experiment. The first field test lasted a full 48 hours. Multiple metal-mesh holding cages containing a total of 1,200 larval sea lampreys collected from local streams were placed throughout the stream as control populations in addition to the creek's already heavily infested larval sea lamprey population.

The field test was conducted with what the HBBS crew called Dowlap 30, a 30% stock solution of 3,4,6-trichloro-2-nitrophenol. The chemical was loaded into the backs of trucks and driven to the banks of Little Billie's Creek in the early morning hours. The yellowish, pungent-smelling chemical was then mixed into a 50-gallon holding tank of water onshore and pumped into the creek at a rate steady enough to maintain a consistent concentration of around 30 ppm. It was reported that more than 96% of the larvae were killed while no nontarget mortalities occurred. As amazing as it must have been, it was still far from a "Eureka!" moment.

"It worked right off the bat," Cliff said, "the minute we starting pumping the chemical into Little Billie's there, the ammocoetes started floating up." Ammocoete is a technical term for a larval lamprey. According to Cliff, when the old gas-powered partitioning pump was fired up and began glugging chemicals into the creek, he saw what he guessed was more 30,000 larval lampreys floating in lifeless masses with the current. Halloween was only a few days away, and this must have been a fitting sight. But Cliff just grinned and shook his head when asked whether there was cheering or any kind of victory dance among the crew. "That just wasn't the type of guys they were," he said. "They didn't get fired up about anything."

Everyone at HBBS knew that there was still a lot of work to do. For starters, maintaining a 30-ppm concentration in the stream to effectively kill the larvae required too much chemical. At these concentrations, it would cost too much to treat the thousands of miles of vascularlike Great Lakes tributaries on a management scale. Of the list of compounds discovered to selectively kill sea lampreys, it was hoped one would be more efficient than Dowlap. The search and refinement process had to push on.

The limits would be tested at HBBS in the following years from 1957 to 1959. Fueled by the promising field tests in 1957, the lab continued to

Cliff Kortman cleans dead larval sea lampreys out of an experimental holding cage in Little Billie's Creek, Millersburg, Michigan, October 29, 1957, as data are recorded onshore. (Photo courtesy Cliff Kortman.)

operate 24 hours a day, seven days a week, with many of the personnel putting in seven-day work weeks. After the hype settled from the test at Little Billie's Creek, the crew would have to wait out the winter before beginning field tests again in 1958.

In 1958 Carp Creek (now called the Black Mallard River), another small Lake Huron tributary just up the road from HBBS, was the next infested stream to receive a test treatment after the spring thaw. This time the test was made public. The HBBS crew, locals, representatives from the Canadian Research Board, and even a few employees from Dow Chemical came to watch. Again metal mesh baskets containing live larvae were placed in the streambed at various locations throughout the entire stream. Wearing a black rubber apron, plastic face shield, and rubber gauntlet gloves, Ben Domke, a pioneering biologist who started work with Cliff, hoisted metal drum after metal drum of liquid Dowlap 20 (a 20% stock solution) and dumped them into a massive washtub to mix with river water during pumping.

This time the chemical was pumped through a perforated tube that was laid across the streambed—a new innovation that allowed the chemical to enter the water more evenly than dumping it in. About an hour into the test, thousands of sickened larval lampreys began emerging from the mud and dying in the chemical tide. All the larvae within the mesh cages were dead within a few hours of pumping. The water of the Black Mallard River has always been rich with leaf tannins due to its heavily wooded watershed. The tannins make the water reddish-brown, like tea that steeped too long. During the treatment in 1958, the addition of Dowlap made the water even more intensely colored. After watching the treatment, a staff writer for a local newspaper wrote, "The waters of the creek, red-hued like the miracle in the story of Moses, may spell deliverance from the scourge of the eel."

Again the hype settled quickly. Predictably, too much chemical had been required to reach and maintain a lethal concentration in the stream. Larger rivers would be impossible to treat.

Back at the station, all attention focused on Cliff's chemical no. 5209—TFM. It was very close in chemical composition to Dowlap, could also be produced in mass quantities, and, according to Cliff's data, seemed to be even more selectively toxic to sea lampreys. I asked Cliff where TFM originally came from, and he explained the original supplier had always been a mystery to him. Companies typically kept chemical formulas hidden from the testing crew to protect patent rights.

Had it not been for a patent rights battle a few years later, the original provider of TFM to HBBS might never have been known. Applegate and Howell had filed for a patent for TFM on April 11, 1957. Otto Scherer, Heinz Frensch, and Gerhard Stähler, officials from Farbwerke Hoechst Aktiengesellschaft whose New York representative was the Progressive Color Company, filed an appeal in 1958. In 1964 Applegate and Howell's TFM patent was appealed in court when it was concluded that Scherer and his colleagues had the original idea for TFM as a lampricide after noticing its similarity to Applegate's other compounds. Applegate had "merely made the test"[26]

Back when 3-bromo-4-nitrophenol (no. 174) was a candidate as a lampricide at HBBS, news of the discovery and subsequent problems with synthesizing the compound made its way into the December 17, 1955, issue of *Chemical Week*. A week later a representative of the Progressive Chemical Company (PCC), Mr. L. C. Balling, sent a letter to Applegate stating that PCC had seen the article on the difficulty of finding a selective toxicant for sea lampreys. He wrote, "We have also noted that your endeavors heretofore for an effective control of lampreys have focused on a chemical compound, viz. 3-bromo-4-nitrophenol, but because of the very high cost of this material your agency is still looking for an effective agent which perhaps could be procured at a reasonable cost." He mentioned that PCC was a representative of a larger company in West Germany, "Farbwerke Hoechst A. G., Frankfurt (Main)," which was "one of the largest chemical manufacturers in that country." He wrote that he had communicated with officials at the company on the topic of lampricides, and, although 3-bromo-4-nitrophenol was too difficult for them to manufacture, "they believe that a similar chemical compound namely 3-trifluormethyl-4-nitrophenol [*sic*] may even be more effective for the purpose you have in mind, and in the event you are interested in this matter we would be very glad to furnish you with free samples of this material."

Applegate was well over capacity with chemicals to test at the time. It took him about a month to reply to Balling's letter, and he almost turned the TFM sample down. "I wish to thank you for your letter of December 29, 1955 in which you offer to provide us with a sample of 3-trifluormethyl-4-nitrophenol [*sic*] for testing as a candidate sea lamprey larvicide," he wrote. "Due to financial limitations and personnel shortages, we have not been accepting further substances for testing." He went on, "However, since we are interested in exploring the structures related to 3-bromo-4-nitrophenol, and since the substance you offer is similar to this compound, we feel that it would be advantageous to work it into our program."

Applegate had to be choosy regarding any new compounds that were going to be added to their already 24/7 testing regime. Thousands of chemicals at HBBS were still stacked on shelves waiting to be tested. In his response to Balling, Applegate wrote that he would need only a small quantity, "about three to four grams," to get a preliminary screening. "If you can arrange to have this amount of 3-trifluormethyl-4-nitrophenol [*sic*] shipped to us, we will be glad to explore its possibilities as a specific larvicide."[27]

A month later a package arrived at HBBS containing a small glass vial of yellowish powder, TFM. The vial was handed to Cliff, and the tests were astounding. The yellow powder could kill larval sea lampreys and not harm other fish at just 2 ppm, more than a sixfold lower concentration than the approximately 13 ppm required using Dowlap. Plans were made to synthesize and ship TFM immediately, and Dow Chemical agreed to do it. The Fish and Wildlife Service, through a special appropriation by the US government, purchased 10,000 pounds of TFM from Dow Chemical in 1958 to prepare for large-scale field tests like never before.

Once bulk shipments of TFM began to arrive at the station, the idea was to rush truckloads of chemical, crews, and equipment up to a few secluded tributaries to Lake Superior in the Upper Peninsula of Michigan for the first tests. The rush up north was primarily fueled by the urgency to save the last wild fish stocks in Lake Superior.

On May 14, 1958, TFM was used in the field for the first time in the Mosquito River. William "Bill" Anderson was just a young technician with the Marquette control office when he found himself loaded up and heading to the Mosquito River application site with the crew. He had wandered over to the Main Street office, "across from Remilard's Bar," to apply for a temporary lamprey control job building electrical weirs in 1956, a decision that led to 37 years as a sea lamprey control biologist.

"It was a rough road going in there," Bill said as we sat with his long-time friend Ralph Wilcox in the Wilcox Fish House and Restaurant near Brimley, Michigan. "We had to use power wagons to get in there because that was in the early spring, the roads were really bad." They finally got all the gear down the narrow, swampy trail to Mosquito River Falls. The falls were a good starting point—an ideal mixing spot at a natural barrier for sea lampreys about two miles upstream from the mouth at Lake Superior.

Bill and the crew mixed up the TFM in a giant bin onshore. They started up the old gas partitioning pump and began pumping it in. "All the big shots were there," Bill chuckled as he recalled the excitement in the air. The HBBS crew, including Applegate and Howell; a few from

Dow Chemical Company employees wearing protective face shields pour Dowlap 30 into a mixing barrel on the banks of Little Billie's Creek, Millersburg, Michigan, October 29, 1957. (Photo courtesy of the Great Lakes Fishery Commission.)

Ann Arbor, including Moffett; sea lamprey control specialists from Ontario, Marquette, and Ludington field stations; and many more were there. "Dr. Applegate was all business most of the time," Bill told me as he talked about the excitement that day. "He was Dr. Applegate."

The treatment was carried out much like the previous field tests with Dowlap: control cages with larvae were placed in the stream, the chemical was pumped in, and the same parameters were measured. Bill will never forget what he saw next. Thousands of sick and dying larval sea lampreys emerged from the streambed. The larvae in the holding cages were also dead. "Oh yeah, it was a good treatment," Bill said. "There was a rainbow overhead at the same time, too." Posttreatment the biologists combed a 1,400-foot stretch of the previously infested Mosquito River with electrofishing gear and found only four larvae. It was estimated that the crew killed more than 99% of the larval sea lampreys during the treatment.[28]

James Moffett (*left*) counts dead sea lamprey larvae laid out on a stump in the Mosquito River, a tributary to Lake Superior in Michigan's Upper Peninsula, while Vern Applegate (*right*) records data, May 14, 1958. They called TFM Lamprecid 2770 at the time. (Photo courtesy of the Great Lakes Fishery Commission.)

"The treatment was an unqualified success," Applegate was quoted as saying in the May 17, 1958, edition of the *Milwaukee Journal.* "The Mosquito River now is completely cleansed of lampreys."[29] It was finally, by all accounts, a Eureka! moment.

As we sat in the restaurant, Ralph told me that the lampricide was applied in tributaries to Lake Superior not a moment too soon. Ralph is a commercial fisherman by trade, but in his later years he also became a restauranteur specializing in lake-to-table Great Lakes fish. He was born in 1942 into a multigenerational tribal commercial-fishing family, a member of the Sault Ste. Marie Tribe of Chippewa Indians, and has served as an adviser to the Great Lakes Fishery Commission since 1984.

"I spent over 60 years fishing the Great Lakes," Ralph said as we ate his famous smoked Lake Superior whitefish dip. "Back to my mother's side on the reservation, that's all they did was fish, and my dad started fishing when he was 13 years old." Ralph remembers the first impact of

Ten-year-old Ralph Wilcox in a boat with his grandfather in 1952. (Photo courtesy Ralph Wilcox.)

sea lampreys along the south shore of Lake Superior well. "It was 1951 when we were lifting lake trout, we were getting a few sea lampreys right at the start," he said, "The next spring, the only thing we got were burbot, and they were all scarred up—very few lake trout."

Whitefish and lake trout vanished. Ralph mentioned that almost all fish caught back then, if they caught any, were scarred and many fishing families thought extinction of whitefish and lake trout was a real possibility. People came in and went out of Ralph and his wife Shirley's restaurant while we sat and chatted about the discovery of TFM. Ralph firmly believes that without this discovery, he would be out of business. "Those people that came here today, the one group, they came here to eat whitefish—they didn't come here to eat anything else," Ralph added.

CHAPTER 6

MULTINATIONAL AIS CONTROL

No time was wasted in applying TFM in both Canadian and US tributaries. Eight additional streams were treated in 1958 while scientists at HBBS tinkered with different formulations of TFM to make it easier to produce. One formula was called Lamprecid 2770, with 45% active ingredient, and the other was one with 30% active ingredient, sometimes referred to as Dowlap F40. The first Ontario tests with TFM were conducted on the Pancake River on August 26 and the West Davignon River on November 5. Over the next several years, treatments with various TFM formulas were carried out regularly on the rivers around Lake Superior. Electrical weirs with integrated traps were used to monitor numbers of migrating adults each spring. In a coordinated effort, all Lake Superior streams with known infestations, as well as a few in Lakes Huron and Michigan, had been treated by the end of 1960.

The lampricide treatments continued each year, but spawning runs of sea lampreys remained high each spring. There were still two generations, two year classes, of parasitic phase sea lampreys out in the lakes, and they were still feeding, growing, and migrating. Infested streams, called producers, were still being discovered, all of which were still adding to the parasitic population in the lakes. Everyone held their breath. Were they wasting hundreds of thousands of dollars on a shot in the dark?

The tides finally turned in 1962. At the Great Lakes Fishery Commission annual meeting, held in Ann Arbor on June 19–20, 1962, Claude Ver Duin, meeting chair and commissioner, stood before the crowd and announced that together they had achieved what was once thought impossible. He reported that the catch of spawning lampreys at electrical barriers in US tributaries of Lake Superior in 1962 was 6,191 compared to 51,628 in 1961. The catch in Canadian tributaries of Lake Superior was 454 compared to 1,555 in 1961. Sea lamprey populations were falling.[1]

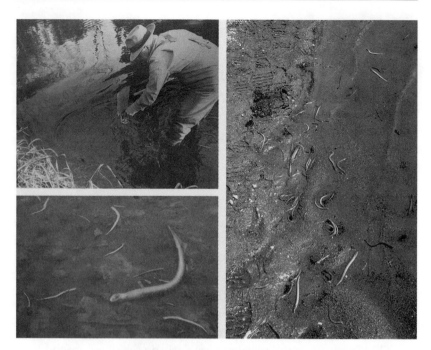

James Moffett collects dead larvae in a can after a successful field test with TFM, c. late 1950s. (Photos courtesy of the Great Lakes Fishery Commission.)

Screening for new compounds to selectively kill lampreys didn't stop after TFM was discovered. Researchers at HBBS were determined to make TFM more efficient both financially and functionally. In the same pickle-jar bioassays used earlier, a new group of compounds, halogenated nitrosalicylanilides, were discovered to selectively kill sea lampreys. One compound in particular, with the trade name Baylucide, or Bayer 73, a well-known mulluscicide used for selective removal of snails around the world known to transmit highly infectious parasitic flatworms to humans (i.e., trematodes of the genus *Schistosoma* and *Fasciola*),[2] was shown to work well as an additive to TFM. A mixture of the two increased the selectivity of the lampricide while reducing the amount of TFM required per treatment. Biologists began adding Bayer 73 to TFM by 1962, and it's still used as an additive today. Eventually, a granular form of Bayer 73 was developed, designed to sink to the bottom and specifically target larval sea lampreys in deeper infested waters with slower currents.

Evolution of Control

Sixty years later sea lamprey control has been going on in tributaries of the Great Lakes long enough for more than three generations of biologists to have spent their careers doing it. Tim Sullivan, a treatment supervisor at the Fish and Wildlife Service's Ludington Biological Station, is a second-generation control biologist by both career and blood. Tim's father, Leo Sullivan, was the first station supervisor in Ludington beginning in the 1950s. "Best job in the world. I'm still convinced to this day that it is," Tim said at the station while thumbing through old photos. Tim grew up seeing his father work in sea lamprey control, went to college with sea lamprey control in mind, and started as a seasonal technician—eventually working his way up to treatment supervisor.

Leo Sullivan was in charge at the Ludington station when lampricide treatments were first determined to be effective. "It wasn't just a paycheck or something like that," Tim mentioned as he recalled his dad telling him that the Great Lakes fishery was bouncing back due to their work. "They really enjoyed being out there in the field—big sacrifices on their part as far as being away from family," Tim told me.

Tim carries on a family tradition of sea lamprey control. "The crew itself is about 17 people altogether, and my job is leadership, oversee the crew," Tim explained. "Generally we go out for a ten-day trip." Sea lamprey control crews like Tim's are based at the Fish and Wildlife Service's biological stations in Ludington (est. 1956) and Marquette (est. 1956) in Michigan and the Department of Fisheries and Oceans Sea Lamprey Control Centre, or SLCC (est. 1966), in Sault Ste. Marie, Ontario. These three control bases are coordinated by the Great Lakes Fishery Commission, are centrally located in the basin, and together carry out sea lamprey control in every corner of the Great Lakes.

Treatments are administered with medical-level accuracy by means of calibrated peristaltic pumps in infested tributaries that feed the Great Lakes. Current resources allow for roughly 200 tributaries to be treated each year; the streams are chosen based on regular surveys for larvae. If and when survey crews find new populations, the new streams are added to the treatment schedule.

The process of administering a treatment has advanced significantly from the early days, but the general approach is still the same. A few biologists arrive at the application site early to begin measur-

Leo Sullivan (*left*) and Bob Weymouth (*right*) of the Ludington Biological Station hand-grab a couple of spawning sea lampreys off nests in Berlinski Creek in 1967. (Photo courtesy of the Great Lakes Fishery Commission.)

ing flow rates. Each river is unique. The banks are sometimes over-grown, and the biologists trudge through briars and poison ivy, up sand dunes, and across cow pastures. Sometimes the waters are cold, fast, and rocky, other times slow and muddy. A convoy of trucks haul-ing trailers pulls into the upstream treatment site to unload lampri-cide and gear.

Nowadays the lampricide comes in plastic jugs with threaded caps, air vents, and handles. In the 1960s, TFM came in 70-pound leaky metal cans. Early control biologists often tell me that the cans were opened like giant beer cans, before they had pull tabs, except the opener was a pickax. Lampricide is still added to a large holding tank onshore for most treatments. From the holding tank, calibrated pumps administer the chemical in the river.

Ontario Department of Fisheries and Oceans Sea Lamprey Control Centre crew members use a helicopter to transport TFM to an application site on the Magnetawan River, which flows into Georgian Bay in Lake Huron, c. 1980. (Photo courtesy of the Great Lakes Fishery Commission.)

Those that worked on the first treatment crews in the 1960s won't deny that lampricide treatments were more likely to kill other fishes back then. It was a primitive operation at the start, which means that sometimes the chemical went into the river a little hot. Most treatments were applied at twice the lethal concentration for larval sea lampreys in an effort to save the remaining fishery back out in the lakes.[3] Early lamprey control biologists often say that most sport fishers and residents around the basin have never forgotten those early nontarget fish kills, and still hold a grudge about it today. Today, treatment crews monitor the concentrations of lampricide at regular intervals throughout the treatment to insure the chemical stays selective.

"The chemical has to be applied at a specific rate at a specific time," Tim Sullivan told me while discussing the sensitivity of the operation. "If you're not able to maintain a consistent concentration, then you can have two things happen: you can be ineffective for actually killing the

In the top photo, biologist Dave Bartell (*left*) pours TFM into a mixing bin on Michigan's Kalamazoo River while biologist Charlie Chambers (*right*) hauls barrels in September 1965. In the bottom photo, control biologists prepare to treat Ontario's Kaministiquia River in 1962. (Photos courtesy of the Great Lakes Fishery Commission.)

lamprey if too weak, or if you're too strong, you can start killing nontargets, which we don't want to do."

TFM and Bayer 73 are registered with the Health Canada Pest Management Regulatory Agency and the US Environmental Protection Agency (EPA) for use as a pesticide. In the years following the publication of *Silent Spring*, a groundbreaking book by Rachel Carson, there came an era of environmental awareness and legislative actions that banned pesticides such as DDT. These actions saved countless species from extinction.

"In 1970, when EPA was formed, one of the first things they did is they looked at some of these chemicals and pesticides that had been previously registered, and they said, 'We don't have enough data,' and one of them was TFM," Rosalie "Roz" Schnick told me as we sat in her home in La Crosse, Wisconsin, in the summer of 2016. "This is what we were here for at the fish control lab," Roz explained. "We had chemists and fishery biologists and all kinds of technical experts." Roz described the research team led by Fred Meyer at the Fish and Wildlife Service's National Fishery Research lab in La Crosse, which worked diligently to screen the compounds for any adverse environmental, ecological, or human effects. During the re-registration process, Roz organized all the data, assembled the literary reviews required for the compounds, and coordinated the process as a liaison between the Fish and Wildlife Service and the EPA. "It took nearly 17 years to re-register TFM and Bayer 73, and it couldn't have happened without a multidisciplinary team of scientists at the La Crosse lab," Roz told me. The data were collected and submitted, the compounds re-registered in 1987, and re-registered again in 1999.[4]

Nontarget mortality can still happen during a stream treatment, but it's rare. The toxicity of TFM and Bayer 73 to sea lampreys and other aquatic organisms is influenced by a suite of factors that need to be constantly monitored, including (1) alkalinity, (2) pH, (3) turbidity, (4) temperature, (5) dissolved oxygen, and (6) the presence of other toxic substances and pollutants.[5] The sensitivity to TFM of mollusks, macroinvertebrates, native lampreys, tadpoles, adult frogs, mudpuppies, and primitive fishes such as juvenile lake sturgeon has been demonstrated in several studies.[6] Crews monitor each treatment closely to watch for nontarget mortalities and adjust treatments when possible to avoid them. Water samples are collected at regular intervals to ensure that lampri-

Ellie Koon teaches fish identification to children during a public Great Lakes sea lamprey control event, c. 1990s. (Photo courtesy of the Great Lakes Fishery Commission.)

cide concentrations stay within the proper range for maximum sea lamprey lethality while remaining harmless to other creatures. Lampricide degrades in sunlight and through microbial decomposition.[7] It takes roughly three days to disappear after application.[8]

Sea lamprey control biologists explore streams and rivers of the Great Lakes Basin that most people have never seen. Every part of the tributary is treated, from tiny feeder creeks that trickle into branches of the main river to backwater sloughs and rapids. Larval sea lampreys aren't safe anywhere. Scientists have developed slow-releasing TFM bars to be placed in difficult to reach areas—hiding places. Occasionally a jug of TFM is dripped in through an adjustable valve into a small creek like an intravenous injection. The main pulse of the lampricide is still administered primarily through a perforated tube stretched across the river. Larval sea lampreys emerge from the streambed when they sense the lampricide and flee downstream with the current. They usually don't get far.

An important difference today is that a treatment crew is no longer all male. Ellie Koon, a biologist recently retired from the Ludington Biological Station, remembers the shift from an all-boys club well. Ellie was one of the first women on a control crew when she started as a summer technician in 1984. "None of this equipment was made for women, and their attitude toward it was 'just suck it up,'" Ellie told me at the Ludington station. She pushed through stereotypes on a daily basis when she started: "There was a lot of discrimination at the time, but I was determined to succeed. I have a hard personality so I didn't let it get to me. . . . I hung in there, and now there are so many women in the program we like to refer to it as the *she lamprey program*, but back then it was a real challenge."

When Ellie started, a lot of the streams around the Great Lakes were still heavily polluted. "Sea lampreys need good water—you don't see sea lamprey in trashy, crummy streams," Ellie pointed out as we looked at an old treatment map. This has created another ironic twist as the battle against sea lampreys continues today. As rivers and streams around the Great Lakes become less polluted, they gradually transition into suitable habitat for sea lampreys. Ellie told me that not all of these are small streams. Then she told me to look into the St. Marys River story.

St. Marys Story

In the early 1990s the St. Marys River, a nearly 75-mile-long binational connection that drains Lake Superior at Whitefish Bay southeast into Lake Huron, had become clean enough to support sea lampreys despite decades of industrial abuse. Larry Schleen was instrumental in dealing with this very big new problem. "I led the [Great Lakes Fishery Commission] task force on the St. Marys River sea lamprey control front," Larry explained at the SLCC in 2015. "Back in the early days, the St. Marys River was heavily polluted," Larry added. "It wasn't even suitable for shad flies." He told me that much of the pollution came from tanneries, smelters, and other industries with lax environmental restrictions.

In 1987, under the international Great Lakes Water Quality Agreement, the St. Marys River was designated an Area of Concern. Tightened environmental regulations led to a gradual increase in water quality, which in turn led to increased larval sea lamprey populations. A spike in sea lamprey destruction in northern Lake Huron followed, and recreational, charter, and commercial fishing groups reacted.

"We did some dye studies to actually simulate a treatment if we could

Cecil Rivers preps a granular Bayer 73 blower mounted on the bow of an aluminum boat to treat larval "hot spots" in the St. Marys River in 1976. (Photo courtesy of the Great Lakes Fishery Commission.)

get to that point." Larry Schleen explained. In reality there wasn't enough money in the entire annual budget to treat even a portion of a river this size. The team turned to detailed habitat assessments and electrofishing gear to locate all areas of high sea lamprey density and relied on helicopters and boats to hit each hot spot with granular Bayer 73.

Back at HBBS, the crew had developed a way to sterilize male sea lampreys.[9] Sterile males were released by the thousands, could still spawn successfully, could still fertilize eggs on nests, and the eggs could still begin the early stages of development, yet the chemosterilant would reliably cause developmental failure around the fifteenth day of incubation.

"It became a real headache," Larry added. Still, the team used every weapon it had on the St. Marys problem, carried it out with military-like coordination, and brought the largest single-river population of sea lampreys ever found in the Great Lakes under control.[10]

There is no evidence that sea lampreys are developing a resistance to TFM or Bayer 73.[11] But scientists can never stop monitoring the situation.[12] We may not always have a lampricide to use against sea lampreys,

Sea lamprey control crews set up for a lampricide treatment in Michigan's Ocqueoc River, just upstream of the sea lamprey control barrier, in 2017. (Photo by the author.)

the main weapon used today, and so the quest to find new control strategies must continue.

Scientific Innovation

It seems evident now that no single control measure, no panacea, mechanical or biological, will prove either effective or practical in reducing the numbers of lampreys. To meet the exigencies of varying stream conditions, of conflicting methods of watershed utilization, and of available financial support, it may be most feasible to employ to some degree, any and every effective method of reducing the numbers of lampreys where local conditions permit their use.[13]

Vernon Applegate spoke these words at the annual meeting of the GLSLC meeting in 1949, and they couldn't have been more prophetic for the program. While TFM and Bayer 73 remain the backbone of the control program, the quest for alternative control methods, and for ways

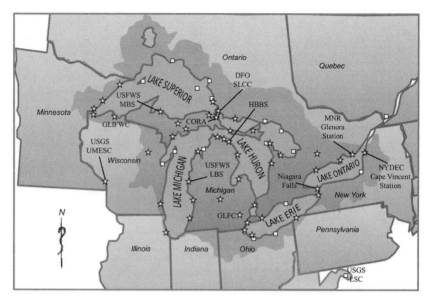

Locations around the Great Lakes discussed in this history. Stars indicate areas visited by author where interviews were conducted and squares indicate areas where interviewees worked, the places they told stories about, or additional key locations in this history. (Map by author, not to scale.)

to integrate multiple methods into the program at once, known as integrated pest management, or IPM, has never slowed.

Barriers and traps are still used regularly today to stop adult migrations and monitor the size of the sea lamprey population by means of tagging studies. Lamprey control wouldn't be possible without them. Barriers allow for a reduction in the amount of lampricide used in stretches upstream of a barrier. To leave no stone unturned, stretches upstream of barriers are still monitored by lamprey control teams with electrofishing gear to determine whether migrating sea lampreys are slipping by. But there is the problem of barriers stopping other important native fishes from completing there migrations. Efforts are under way to develop barriers that stop sea lampreys yet allow other fishes to complete their upstream migrations.[14] Meanwhile, some low-head weirs, often used in combination with electricity and traps, allow some fishes like salmon to jump over while still stopping sea lampreys, which can't jump.

An era of pheromone exploration is under way, and is where I started my career with sea lampreys. New pheromone components, the unique chemical language of sea lampreys, are being identified and synthesized. The compounds are environmentally benign, can manipulate the movements of migrating and spawning sea lampreys, and can be applied to sea lamprey control in the Great Lakes, as well as conservation programs in their native range.

Researchers recently identified an alarm cue, a concentrated smell of dead sea lampreys that repels migrating individuals in streams, creating another possible management tool.[15] The genome of the sea lamprey was recently revealed, giving us full access to the animal's genetic codes.[16] A quick Google Scholar search with the phrase "sea lamprey control" now yields nearly 26,000 hits in 0.07 seconds. The quest for alternative control methods has never slowed—it can't.

CONCLUSION

The sea lamprey was the first AIS that we took action against in the Great Lakes, the only one controlled through binational intervention, and the only one in the Great Lakes still under control today. The lampricide discovery was the first of its kind for an aquatic vertebrate, the result of decades of dedicated science directed at species-specific vulnerabilities.

So what if the sea lamprey control program simply stopped? This is a central question that arose again and again during my research trips around the lakes. I began asking this question to Great Lakes sea lamprey control biologists in both the United States and Ontario. Those with a lifetime of experience dealing with this invader.

"That's a good question," Doug Cuddy chuckled as we talked at the SLCC in Sault Ste. Marie, Ontario. Doug started working at the SLCC as a biologist in the spring of 1970, just a few years after salmon were stocked in the Great Lakes. "Sea lamprey control was vital to get the chinook, coho, and other salmon fisheries up and running," he said.

Doug mentioned that many around the Great Lakes still remember what it was like when salmon were planted in the lower lakes before sea lamprey control began in Lakes Erie and Ontario. Naturally, I wanted to know more about sea lampreys and the early salmon days. Was sea lamprey control vital to establishing salmon in the Great Lakes for a recreational fishery? I tracked down a fisheries biologist that experienced salmon-stocking attempts before sea lamprey control firsthand.

John Heinrich spent his career in Great Lakes sea lamprey control, including work at HBBS and the Marquette Biological Station, but his first fisheries job was in the summer of 1972 at the New York Department of Environmental Conservation (NYDEC) Cape Vincent Fisheries Station. The station is situated at the entrance of the St. Lawrence River in eastern Lake Ontario. Lampricide treatments in Lake Ontario began

Sept. 22, 1969
Chinook "Jack"
Ocqueoc River
Salmon
24.8 inches
6 lbs-13 oz.

A Chinook salmon that was captured in the Ocqueoc River just one year after salmon were stocked in Lake Huron near Rogers City, Michigan. (Photo courtesy of the Great Lakes Fishery Commission.)

at the same time—in 1971 on the Canadian side (23 tributaries treated), and 1972 on the US side along the south shore (20 tributaries treated).[1]

John told me that Pacific salmon were being stocked in Lake Ontario by the hundreds of thousands, but the returns had been grim. "Biologists were bringing the fish that they caught back to the Cape Vincent, New York, fishery station," John said as we chatted at his home in Antigo, Wisconsin, in 2016. "Twenty [scars] per fish—it actually looked like they were shot with a shotgun." The salmon that did manage to return to attempt a spawning run were malnourished. "These were salmon that should have weighed 20 pounds; they were only 6 to 7 pounds— somehow some of them still survived," John said. After a few years of sea lamprey control in major producer tributaries of the lower Great Lakes, salmon became healthy, and a healthy recreational fishery followed.

All of the sea lamprey control biologists with whom I spoke, both retired and currently working, explained that sea lamprey control is vital to the health of the Great Lakes fishery. But do current fisheries managers feel the same way? Sea lampreys are mostly out of sight in the Great

Lakes, so one can reason that they must be out of mind. I traveled to the Cape Vincent station that John mentioned to find out.

Steve LaPan is the Great Lakes section head for the NYDEC based at the historic Cape Vincent Fisheries station. "The impact of sea lamprey, I think, is largely underestimated by most people," Steve told me as we sat in his office. "Most people around the lakes don't know sea lamprey control is going on," he added. "Sea lamprey control is in our backyard, it's virtually going on in everyone's backyard whether they know it or not . . . The problem is persistent all the way from the eastern end of Lake Ontario up through all of the upper lakes and down Lake Michigan into the Chicago area."

Across the St. Lawrence River from the Cape Vincent station, Andy Todd has been the OMNR's Lake Ontario Management Unit fisheries manager since 2009. The NYDEC and OMNR offices work together with partners to manage the Lake Ontario fishery. Andy and Steve both told me that it's difficult for fisheries managers of this generation to consider what would happen if sea lamprey control ceased, as the species has been controlled for so long. Every management decision they make today hinges on sea lampreys being under control. "People, including managers, forget the impact of sea lamprey control and the devastation that it played on our fisheries," Andy added as we talked about the healthy recreational fishery throughout the basin. Andy noted that fisheries managers today must consider sea lamprey control in all their decision making.

Indeed, the recreational fishery is booming not just in the eastern basin of Lake Ontario but across the Great Lakes, in both Canada and the United States. It made me wonder, what does the recreational fishing community have to say about sea lamprey control?

Mike Miller grew up in southern Ontario, on the shores of Lake Ontario, and hunted and fished along the shores of the Great Lakes as a kid. Now he hosts and produces OFAH's award-winning *Angler & Hunter Television*. "My roots are in Ontario, Lake Ontario and its tributaries," Mike told me in OFAH's Hunting and Fishing Heritage Centre in Peterborough in 2017.

Mike told me that right around the time he began fishing seriously, alewives became a problem in Lake Ontario. This was also when the first stocking programs for Pacific salmon began in Lake Ontario. Mike and I talked about early salmon stocking, how salmon grew very fast, and ate a lot of alewives, and how a booming sport-fishing industry grew out of all of it. "I think a lot of people became avid salmon fishermen after that," Mike said. He was quick to point out that sea lampreys are still out there and the sport-fishing community still deals with this AIS. "As an angler, one of the things that I encounter fishing in the lakes and rivers is invasive species," Mike said. "Whether you're scouting creeks or trolling for salmon in the Great Lakes, you do encounter sea lampreys," he added. "Based on the fish that I've caught over the years with scars and open sores on them . . . I imagine it would be a real big problem if they weren't managed."

Matt DeMille, manager of fish and wildlife services with OFAH and sport-fishing adviser for Ontario to the Great Lakes Fishery Commission, joined the conversation at the OFAH headquarters. "Sea lamprey control is kind of a new normal," Matt said. "We've been controlling sea lamprey for so long that people can take that for granted." He explained the importance of educational outreach, in both the fisheries community and the general public, related to the sea lamprey control program—and how, like sea lamprey control itself, education and public outreach are an ongoing effort.

Sea lamprey control education and outreach are gaining momentum around the lakes. Sea lamprey information and displays are found at most commercial fishing and Great Lakes museums I've visited. Displays and outreach booths show up at major sport-fishing shows and tournaments, marinas, and other boat landings here and there. Education about sea lampreys also happens between clients and charter captains while they are out on the lakes fishing. My next stop was to talk to them.

I made my way to Grand Haven, Michigan. Along the docks at the Grand Isle Marina, where the Grand River empties into Lake Michigan, charter and recreational fishing boats were lined up as far as I could see. It was dawn over Lake Michigan as I walked along the docks, and the low putter of a fishing boat filled with laughing clients echoed in the distance as they motored out of the marina. Captain Denny Grinold waved hello on the other side of the dock.

"Well, I became a charter boat captain in 1983," Denny said as we sipped coffee next to his 33-foot custom-built charter fishing boat *Old Grin* in 2017. Denny explained that charter fishing on the Great Lakes draws clients from all over the Midwest and beyond, and questions about sea lampreys almost always come up while they are out on the water.

"A charter boat is a platform that you can fish on, [and] we provide that platform," Denny said, "It's for people that have neither the means nor the time to maintain a boat, equipment for fishing, and the rest that goes with it—they can simply rent a charter boat and still have that Great Lakes fishing experience." There's no denying our natural attraction to fishing, a certain excitement that Denny explained "draws us to the water." He said that the idea of catching trophy fish is part of the reason why we go fishing, but another part is the camaraderie and escapism. "You're out there, you're making friends, you're away from the phones, the internet, the traffic, the business, and so forth—fishing provides an atmosphere that's totally relaxing and enjoyable, and exciting, and fun."

I first visited with Denny in 2016 on an earlier research trip when John Robertson, retired chief of the Fisheries and Forest Management divisions of the Michigan DNR, joined us to chat about sea lampreys at the marina. "I started working for the department in 1964 as a research biologist," John said. "Then I worked with the salmon-stocking program in the Great Lakes." John conducted surveys of the first Pacific salmon spawning runs in the Great Lakes in 1966. "People who had never fished in their life were attracted to these fish." He noted that it had only been a few years since sea lampreys were brought under control at that point.

I learned from talking to John and Denny that even though Pacific salmon are not native to the Great Lakes the introduction of these sport fish brought people back to the water and Great Lakes angling and substantially increased their awareness of sea lamprey control. "The foundation of the Great Lakes fishery is based upon sea lamprey control," Denny chimed in. "Without sea lamprey control we wouldn't have a discussion on Asian carp, we wouldn't have a discussion on invasive mussels, we wouldn't have a discussion on salmon stocking, and we wouldn't have a discussion on lake trout restoration." As we sat on a bench in the sun, we agreed we wouldn't have a charter-fishing industry either.

While visiting mainly small fishing towns like Grand Haven, I began to think about major Great Lakes cities. I wondered whether people were fishing again in cities around the lakes and whether they are aware of the sea lamprey control program. I made my way to Chicago, the largest city on the Great Lakes, to find out.

It was a cold, rainy, August day in Chicago when I met and had a beer with Ed Makauskas. "I have been a sport fisherman on Lake Michigan since the late '60s when salmon were introduced to the Great Lakes," Ed told me. We talked for a while about his early fishing adventures in Platte Bay in northeastern Lake Michigan, about renting a 14-foot trihaul boat with a nine-horsepower motor to brave the Great Lakes waters in search of salmon, and about his first experiences catching them.

"Prior to the salmon fishery, Lake Michigan was primarily a perch fishery and a herring fishery," Ed said as he talked about anglers lining up along the Lake Michigan shoreline in Chicago in pursuit of these species. Ed mentioned he was a sport-fishing adviser to the Great Lakes Fishery Commission representing the state of Illinois for 34 years. Throughout my research, several individuals I interviewed served, or currently serve, as advisers to the commission. The Great Lakes Fisheries Act of 1956 appointed advisers from both the United States and Canada to represent interest groups in all jurisdictions around the lakes. "[There was] a sport fishing adviser, a commercial fishing adviser, and a public at large adviser to represent the people who don't actually fish but still have a stake in the fishery and the Great Lakes," Ed said.

Advisers from each jurisdiction around the Great Lakes assist the commissioners in making informed decisions in support of the Great Lakes Fishery Commission's objectives: to work together, control sea lampreys, and improve and perpetuate this fishery. Advisers in the US waters of the lakes are selected from a list provided by the Great Lakes state governors. For Ontario waters, the minister of Fisheries and Oceans Canada appoints advisers based on recommendations from the Ontario Ministry of Natural Resources and Forestry.

"No matter where you went, back in the late '60s, early '70s, it was *coho fever*," Ed laughed. "The papers and the news media in Chicago had photographs of salmon, schools of salmon, up and down the lakes." He told me that sea lampreys caught coho fever as well. "I remember seeing lampreys on trout, and I remember seeing lampreys on salmon," he added. "I think the lamprey will be here forever. And I believe that, unless we control them forever they'll be a devastating force on the Great Lakes."

While in Chicago, I heard about another Great Lakes sport-fishing enthusiast from the area. Don Dubin is a taxidermist, fish carver, and freshwater fishing hall of famer who has lived in Chicago his whole life. As he had no association with the Great Lakes Fishery Commission, I was curious to hear his thoughts about sea lampreys.

"The sea lampreys are still out there," Don explained as we sat in his personal museum of fishing artifacts. I learned that Don helped found the Illinois chapter of Salmon Unlimited in the early 1970s, and has walked to his favorite city piers alongside roaring downtown Chicago for decades to fish Lake Michigan. "It's so important that people make sure that we don't lose the ability to control sea lampreys," Don told me. "Hopefully this will create a fishery for years, and years, and years to come, so my kids' kids will enjoy the fishery that I enjoyed as a young kid."

Most of those who go charter fishing and sport fishing on the Great Lakes today bring back their catches to eat. But not everyone around the Great Lakes has the means to hire a charter boat or access to fishing equipment and boats. Historically, lake-to-table diners and commercial fisheries were scattered all over the Great Lakes Basin, providing fresh fish locally and for export. While local fish is harder to find in cities and towns around the lakes today, a few purveyors remain. I wanted to know what sea lamprey control means for restaurants and whether eating local fish has been making a comeback in the decades since lamprey control began.

The next morning I got up early to visit Steve LaHaie, the manager at Shaw's Crab House on East Hubbard in downtown Chicago. Steve has managed this particular restaurant for more than 30 years. At the center of the spacious interior is one of the most impressive oyster bars in the country. But not everyone comes to Shaw's for the oyster bar, or *bah*, as Steve pointed out.

Steve's grandfather and great-grandfather were both commercial fishermen on the Great Lakes. "The main thing that they caught were whitefish," he told me as we sat at a high-top table before opening hours. "I was young, but I still remember my [grandfather's] open-face whitefish sandwich." Steve told me that those lake-to-table meals as a kid still inspire him today.

On the Shaw's menu you can find wild swordfish, yellowfin tuna, and an impressive spread of live oysters from coastal waters around the United States, but Steve quickly pointed out the walleye and yellow perch from Canadian Great Lakes commercial fisheries and whitefish caught in the US waters of Lake Superior—all of which are popular in the city. "Locally caught organic fish tastes better to me," Steve said, and "it's also better for the environment." Steve didn't talk a lot about the importance of sea lamprey control, although he remembers his father talking about these creatures. Steve mentioned he's never seen one in the wild.

Then our food arrived—Great Lakes yellow perch fillets and broiled whitefish with tomato chutney—a dish inspired by Steve's father's famous broiled whitefish. "He served it with stewed tomatoes," Steve pointed out. I'll never forget how good it tasted.

Many tribal and First Nations fisheries still persist around the Great Lakes. Great Lakes fish are part of their livelihoods and culture. Tribal fisheries continue to catch Great Lakes fishes for subsistence, local markets, and distribution to restaurants and grocery stores around the basin, including places in large cities like Shaw's. So what does sea lamprey control mean to the first Great Lakes fishing families today? I set out 450 miles north from Chicago to Odanah, Wisconsin, to visit the Great Lakes Indian Fish and Wildlife Commission (GLIFWC) office to find out.

"Well, we were known as the Gillnetter Tribe," Ervin Soulier said as we chatted in the GLIFWC conference room. "The fish were usually brought home for tribal consumption." Ervin is a retired natural resources manager for the Bad River Band of Lake Superior Chippewa and a Bad River tribal member. He pointed out that he helped coordinate sea lamprey control efforts in the Bad River, a tributary of Lake Superior more than 70 miles long. The Bad River has been a sea lamprey producer for decades.

"The tribe was reluctant to allow lampricide treatments at first," Ervin explained as we talked about the early control days and nontarget fish kills. Ervin's parents were of the generation that hadn't yet been given US citizenship, under the Indian Citizenship Act of 1924. When he was growing up the United States had not yet acknowledged the tribal fishing rights within waters of the Great Lakes guaranteed by an 1836 treaty.[2] Many tribal members of Ervin's generation were barred from exercising their Lake Superior fishing rights, and therefor did not witness sea lamprey destruction to the fishery, during the peak of the lamprey infestation. Today GLIFWC conservation officials are key partners in the fight against sea lampreys.

Bill Mattes, the GLIFWC Great Lakes section leader and representative to the Great Lakes Fishery Commission, joined us at the table to chat about sea lamprey control.[3] "During my 20-plus years here at the GLIFWC, we have seen ups and downs in the sea lamprey population,"

Bill said. He told us that the importance of sea lamprey control for tribal fisheries was made clear a few decades ago by means of an unintended "experiment." A decision was made by the commission and all its partners to try to cut back on the use of TFM in the lakes.

"We saw an increase in the abundance of sea lamprey, and, as a result we saw declines in the lake trout population." Bill explained that sea lamprey populations made a quick rebound during the lampricide application cutback: "Declines in the lake trout population led directly to declines in the harvest quota, [and] declines in the harvest quota have a direct impact upon the tribal commercial fisherman." Bill told me that tribal commercial fishers not only catch lake trout but they also catch whitefish, and the amount of net they can set is dependent on how many lake trout there are in the population. In short, the decline in the lake trout population due to increased lamprey predation meant a smaller quota for whitefish. At the same time, sport-fishing groups, fishing charters, and commercial fishing operations were also impacted by the increase in scarring and the reduction in salmon, lake trout, and whitefish. In response, the commission and its partners reestablished regular lampricide treatments.

Next, as I headed into the Upper Peninsula of Michigan, I drove east to the Chippewa Ottawa Resource Authority (CORA) office in Sault Ste. Marie for more perspectives on sea lamprey control today.

"Well, of the first wave [of Great Lakes invasive species]—sea lampreys, alewives, and smelt—sea lampreys were probably most notable," Tom Gorenflo, director of the Intertribal Fisheries and Assessment Program told me as we talked at the CORA office. "If there were no sea lamprey control, we wouldn't be here right now, simple as that," he added.

Tom confirmed that since sea lamprey control is a successful program, sea lampreys are less of a concern for intertribal fisheries these days. Newer species, such as invasive mussels, are a different story.

"Invasive mussels are game changers in my opinion, absolute game changers," Tom said while discussing the future of the lakes. "When you can look down in the lake in midsummer and see 60 feet down, that's not good." Concerns about dreissenid mussels are shared by all stakeholder groups and the public across the lakes today, but those that fish for a living are particularly worried.

In Blind River, Ontario, a small town situated on the North Channel of Lake Huron, Brian Nyman and his 93-year-old father, Leonard, were firing up their commercial fishing tug, the *Ellen N*, for a day of fishing in 2017. It was a muggy June morning, just about 5:00 a.m. The engine's low rumble rattled the metal doors on the 55-year-old vessel that Leonard and his brother built by hand. I hopped aboard.

"The whole ecosystem has just totally changed from when my father started fishing," Bryan told me as crew members began to show up and load gear. "We have zebra mussels now, we have quagga mussels, we still have sea lampreys, we have the rainbow smelt, there's the Asian carp threat that we have all the time."

While the Nymans don't see many sea lampreys today, they do see a lot of invasive mussels. "These [AIS] all affect the way the fish act," Bryan said. He went on to explain that AIS are making fishing more difficult with each new invasion. "The whitefish fishery has changed drastically because they're changing their diet." In short, because the whitefish are sustaining themselves on new prey (mainly invasive mussels), they are also changing their behavior, and it's making them both malnourished and harder to catch.

Whitefish are spreading out and searching more for food, are forced to eat invasive mussels with lower nutritional content, and are no longer schooling up as densely as they used to. "What the dreissenid mussels have done is they've cleared the water up, so the sunlight penetrates right to the bottom," Bryan added. "It grows algae on the bottom." Bryan explained that whitefish are avoiding the clearly visible scum-covered nets, and their catches are dropping because of it.

Leonard still fishes most days with his son. "Commercial fisherman all my life, since 1937," he told me. "This was in the Depression, the first Depression way back in the 1900s," he added with a chuckle. Leonard told some of the earliest stories I've heard about fishing the Great Lakes: how he started with his father, how all the fishing was done by hand, how they built their wooden boats. "There was lots of muscle back then," Leonard added as he grinned at his son. He also talked about some of the hardships they faced during the first wave of AIS. "For a period of time, fishing got so bad in the '40s—I think in 1940, just before I got married—I took up flying. I got my pilot's license, and flew for about five years." Leonard spent over 80 years of his life fishing the Great Lakes and observed many changes in the fishery. Yet even the most seasoned commercial fishers like Leonard worry about the future of the lakes' fishery and AIS today.

Next, heading south toward Ann Arbor along the western shores of Lake Huron, I made a detour into the Thumb area of Michigan. In the town of Bay Port overlooking Saginaw Bay, commercial fishing families have persisted since the mid-1800s. The Bay Port Fish Company was established in 1895; Tod Williams and his family have owned it since 1978. Tod told me that the first sea lamprey he saw in Lake Huron was attached to a whopper of a common carp in the 1970s. Sea lampreys were under control in Lake Huron when Tod started fishing, but the water and fishing have changed substantially since then due to newer AIS introductions. While I paged through old fishing photos in Tod's office, he confirmed his concern over invasive mussels and the clearing waters of the Great Lakes and mentioned that sea lampreys are rarely seen these days. He noted that he wouldn't want to know what would happen if sea lamprey control ceased to exist.

The Bay Port Fish Company fishes today much the same way that Beatrice Skaggs's family did in the 1940s. They fish a modern version of the deepwater trap net, the fish are all still alive when lifted into the boat, and they provide local markets with the freshest Lake Huron whitefish. Today the trap net boats are no longer wooden, and substantially fewer sea lampreys are cut up on deck.

After completing my research trips around the lakes, the answer to my question was clear: no sea lamprey control, no fishery. While traveling and collecting stories I thought often of the trip that John Van Oosten and Fred Westerman took in 1937. Eighty years ago the two Great Lakes scientists set out to talk to the people connected with the Great Lakes fishery, record their firsthand knowledge about the lakes, and learn about the impending sea lamprey threat. My charge was the same, just 60 years after sea lampreys were brought under control. I wondered what Van Oosten and Westerman, and all the early scientists, would think of sea lamprey control today. What would Rachel Carson think of the program or the use of lampricide to control these creatures? What would they say about the new AIS threats we face?

Most of the early Great Lakes scientists were retiring around the time polluted rivers were catching fire and alewife die-offs were littering beaches. Things must have looked grim. In the meantime, cities were growing around the lakes with their backs to the water. Now we live in an era in which Great Lakes health is a priority and fish populations are, for the most part, healthy.

The story of sea lamprey control is more than a fish story. It is a reminder of why natural things are important and how each ecosystem is connected. Thinking about the sea lamprey reminds us of our ability to disrupt those ecosystems through our actions and how our actions can also restore and protect those ecosystems once considered lost.

If you visit the Great Lakes and walk along their shores, you will no doubt feel a sense of smallness. No signs of land can be seen as you motor along any one of the five lakes. The lakes account for 20% of Earth's surface freshwater—our most valuable resource. Lake Michigan alone spans more than 300 miles from north to south, and Lake Superior can reach depths of over 1,000 feet, deeper than three California coastal redwoods stacked end to end. It's hard for anyone, including myself, to fully appreciate a freshwater ecosystem of this scale.

Toward the end of writing this book, my wife Devin and I had our one-year wedding anniversary. To celebrate we took a trip to California to visit the coastal redwoods. While walking along the trails in the Muir Woods National Monument, we both seemed to simultaneously experience the same feelings. We felt deep reverence for these towering natural wonders. We were humbled by their size and level of protection. And, oddly, we both thought about the Great Lakes.

Water is precious and scarce along California's central coast, yet these towering ancient trees survive. With a surprisingly shallow root system, the giant redwoods rely on coastal fog, which accumulates and trickles down to provide nearly 40% of their water intake. These tremendous evergreens have an average life-span of around 600 years and can grow more than 300 feet high.

An estimated 1.2 million people walk the trails of Muir Woods annually. Of the thousands that visit each day, no one is talking, some whisper, others just sit. Signs tell visitors to stay on the trail and not litter. The air is heavy, cool, and silent. Everyone is feeling small. The experience brings about thoughts: "how could we have exploited these?" and "thank goodness we saved some." It's a moment when nature reduces us, when we feel more within nature than above it. It reminds us of our responsibility to protect natural things for generations beyond us. We both quickly realized that we've felt the same way, many times, while wandering around the Great Lakes.

The Great Lakes are more than glacial excavations filled with water. They are unique, living, flowing systems filled with creatures and mys-

The author in the Ocqueoc River with a sea lamprey in hand. (Photo by Andrea Miehls, Great Lakes Fishery Commission and US Geological Survey.)

terious shipwrecks. They motivate us to paddle them, dive them, swim across them, and fish them. People travel thousands of miles just to camp and hike Great Lakes dunes and walk along Great Lakes shorelines in search for ancient fossils. Sixty million people visit the Great Lakes each year.

The Great Lakes are freshwater wonders of the world, yet their vastness does not exempt them from deserving our protection. We allowed sea lampreys and other AIS to enter the lakes, and that can't be reversed. The lakes will never again be the way they were, but we can still fight to keep these waters wild and unique. Understanding the importance of sea lamprey control is part of that fight. Learning from our past AIS mistakes to better prevent future introductions is another part, as is voting in support of healthy Great Lakes and supporting programs like the Great Lakes Restoration Initiative, the largest federal investment for Great Lakes health in the last several decades.[4] But I would argue that visiting and enjoying the Great Lakes, and passing that appreciation on, is part of it too.

NOTES

Preface

1. USGS (United States Geological Survey), "Common Carp (*Cyprinus carpio*) Fact Sheet," accessed October 10, 2018, https://nas.er.usgs.gov/queries/factsheet.aspx?speciesID=4

2. Luis Zambrano, Enrique Martínez-Meyer, Naercio Menezes, and A. Townsend Peterson, "Invasive potential of common carp (*Cyprinus carpio*) and Nile tilapia (*Oreochromis niloticus*) in American freshwater systems," *Canadian Journal of Fisheries and Aquatic Sciences* 63, no. 9 (2006): 1903–10.

3. Luis E. Escobar et al., "Aquatic Invasive Species in the Great Lakes Region: An Overview," *Reviews in Fisheries Science & Aquaculture* 26, no. 1 (2018): 121–38.

Introduction: A Biological Invader

1. GLSLC (Great Lakes Sea Lamprey Committee), "Great Lakes Sea Lamprey Committee Meeting Minutes, December 13, 1950," 26, Great Lakes Fishery Commission Archives, Ann Arbor, Michigan.

2. GLLTSLC (Great Lakes Lake Trout and Sea Lamprey Committee), "Great Lakes Lake Trout and Sea Lamprey Committee Meeting Minutes," December 16, 1952, 40, Great Lakes Fishery Commission Archives, Ann Arbor, Michigan.

3. GLSLC (Great Lakes Sea Lamprey Committee), "Report by William J. Harth in the Great Lakes Sea Lamprey Committee Meeting Minutes, 1949," Great Lakes Fishery Commission Archives, Ann Arbor, Michigan.

4. All extant species of lampreys have seven pairs of gills that were thought to look like "eyes," along with actual eyes and the single nasal opening, earning them the name *Neunauge*, a German word meaning "nine-eye."

5. Rickard Bjerselius et al., "Direct Behavioral Evidence That Unique Bile Acids Released by Larval Sea Lamprey (*Petromyzon marinus*) Function as a Migratory Pheromone," *Canadian Journal of Fisheries and Aquatic Sciences* 57, no. 3 (2000): 557–69.

6. Michael C. Wagner, Michael B. Twohey, and Jared M. Fine, "Conspecific

Cueing in the Sea Lamprey: Do Reproductive Migrations Consistently Follow the Most Intense Larval Odour?," *Animal Behaviour* 78, no. 3 (2009): 593–99.

7. Nicholas S. Johnson et al., "A Synthesized Pheromone Induces Upstream Movement in Female Sea Lamprey and Summons Them into Traps," *Proceedings of the National Academy of Sciences* 106, no. 4 (2009): 1021–26.

8. Yu-Wen Chung-Davidson et al., "A Thermogenic Secondary Sexual Character in Male Sea Lamprey," *Journal of Experimental Biology* 216, no. 14 (2013): 2702–12.

9. Simon Henry Gage, *The Lake and Brook Lampreys of New York, Especially Those of Cayuga and Seneca Lakes* (New York: Comstock, 1893), 460.

10. Stephen Smith and Ellen Marsden, "Factors Affecting Sea Lamprey Egg Survival," *North American Journal of Fisheries Management* 29, no. 4 (2009): 859–68.

11. G. J. Farmer, F. W. H. Beamish, and G. A. Robinson, "Food Consumption of the Adult Landlocked Sea Lamprey, *Petromyzon marinus*, L.," *Comparative Biochemistry and Physiology*, part A: *Physiology* 50, no. 4 (1975): 753–57.

12. Andrzej Ciereszko et al., "Factors Affecting Motility Characteristics and Fertilizing Ability of Sea Lamprey Spermatozoa," *Transactions of the American Fisheries Society* 131, no. 2 (2002): 193–202.

13. Tyler Buchinger, email conversation with the author, April 20, 2018.

14. Philip J. Sawyer, "Laboratory Care and Feeding of Larval Lampreys," *Copeia*, no. 3 (1957): 244.

15. Ella Davies, "Blood-Sucking Fish Feed on Whales," *BBC Earth News*, January 3, 2011, http://news.bbc.co.uk/earth/hi/earth_news/newsid_9281000/9281424.stm

16. F. W. H. Beamish, "Biology of the North American Anadromous Sea Lamprey, *Petromyzon marinus*," *Canadian Journal of Fisheries and Aquatic Sciences* 37, no. 11 (1980): 1924–43.

17. K. H. Nislow and Boyd E. Kynard, "The Role of Anadromous Sea Lamprey in Nutrient and Material Transport between Marine and Freshwater Environments," *American Fisheries Society Symposium* 69 (2009): 485–94.

18. Robert W. Gess, Michael I. Coates, and Bruce S. Rubidge, "A Lamprey from the Devonian Period of South Africa," *Nature* 443, no. 7114 (2006): 981.

19. Claude B. Renaud, *Lampreys of the World: An Annotated and Illustrated Catalogue of Lamprey Species Known to Date* (Rome: Food and Agriculture Organization of the United Nations, 2011).

20. J. H. Youson and E. W. Sidon, "Lamprey Biliary Atresia: First Model System for the Human Condition?," *Cellular and Molecular Life Sciences* 34, no. 8 (1978): 1084–86.

21. Chu-Yin Yeh et al., "Intestinal Synthesis and Secretion of Bile Salts as an Adaptation to Developmental Biliary Atresia in the Sea Lamprey," *Proceedings of the National Academy of Sciences* 109, no. 28 (2012): 11419–24.

22. "FBI Cites Crime Rate Rise." *Toledo Blade*, March 10, 1965.

Chapter 1: An Ailing Ecosystem

1. Charles W. Creaser, "The Establishment of the Atlantic Smelt in the Upper Waters of the Great Lakes." *Papers of the Michigan Academy of Science, Arts, and Letters* 5, no. 2 (1925): 406.

2. Stanford H. Smith, "Species succession and fishery exploitation in the Great Lakes," *Journal of the Fisheries Board of Canada* 25, no. 4 (1968): 667–693.

3. For more information, see the websites http://stopaquatichitchhikers.org/ and http://www.invadingspecies.com/invaders/

4. Thomas F. Nalepa, Steven A. Pothoven, and David L. Fanslow, "Recent Changes in Benthic Macroinvertebrate Populations in Lake Huron and Impact on the Diet of Lake Whitefish (*Coregonus clupeaformis*)," *Aquatic Ecosystem Health and Management* 12, no. 1 (2009): 2–10.

5. US Department of Agriculture Economic Research Service, *The Agricultural Situation in the Soviet Union: Review of 1973 and Outlook for 1974*, USDA ERS-Foreign 358, Washington, DC, March 1974, 3; Mark J. Penn, "America Gets the Shaft," *Harvard Crimson*, November 16, 1973, https://www.thecrimson.com/article/1973/11/16/america-gets-the-shaft-pthe-1972/

6. Tom Ford and John Lis, "Monroe Water Emergency Closes Schools, Restaurants," *Toledo Blade*, December 16, 1989, 1.

7. Tom Nalepa, conversation with the author, October 19, 2018.

8. Nalepa, Pothoven, and Fanslow, "Recent Changes in Benthic Macroinvertebrate Populations," 3.

9. GLNPO (Great Lakes National Program Office), US Environmental Protection Agency, "Type E Botulism Outbreaks: A Manual for Beach Managers and the Public," accessed August 10, 2018, http://www.miseagrant.umich.edu/files/2012/10/BotulismManual2012.pdf

10. Schuyler J. Sampson, John H. Chick, and Mark A. Pegg, "Diet Overlap among Two Asian Carp and Three Native Fishes in Backwater Lakes on the Illinois and Mississippi Rivers," *Biological Invasions* 11, no. 3 (2009): 483–96.

11. Garret Ellison, "Asian Carp Caught Near Lake Michigan Got Past Electric Barriers," *MLive*, August 2017, https://www.mlive.com/news/index.ssf/2017/08/asian_carp_caught_near_lake_mi.html

12. See the website of the Asian Carp Regional Coordinating Committee, accessed November 15, 2018, http://www.asiancarp.us/

13. See the website of Ontario's Invading Species Awareness Program, accessed November 15, 2018, http://www.invadingspecies.com/invaders/; Great Lakes Aquatic Nonindigenous Species Information System, accessed November 15, 2018, https://www.glerl.noaa.gov/glansis/

14. R. C. Halliday, "Marine Distribution of the Sea Lamprey (*Petromyzon marinus*) in the Northwest Atlantic," *Canadian Journal of Fisheries and Aquatic Sciences* 48, no. 5 (1991): 832–42.

15. P. S. Maitland, "Review of the Ecology of Lampreys in Northern Europe," *Canadian Journal of Fisheries and Aquatic Sciences* 37, no. 11 (1980): 1944–52.

16. J. H. Youson, "Morphology and Physiology of Lamprey Metamorphosis," *Canadian Journal of Fisheries and Aquatic Sciences* 37, no. 11 (1980): 1687–1710.

17. The Susquehanna River is a tributary of the Atlantic Ocean within the native range of sea lampreys.

18. The Oswego River is a major tributary of Lake Ontario.

19. Randy L. Eshenroder, "The Role of the Champlain Canal and Erie Canal as Putative Corridors for Colonization of Lake Champlain and Lake Ontario by Sea Lampreys," *Transactions of the American Fisheries Society* 143, no. 3 (2014): 634–49.

20. A. H. Lawrie, "The Sea Lamprey in the Great Lakes," *Transactions of the American Fisheries Society* 99, no. 4 (1970): 766–75.

21. Lola T. Dees, "Sea Lampreys of the Atlantic Coast and Great Lakes," Fishery Leaflet 360, US Department of the Interior, Washington, DC (1950): 1.

22. Eshenroder, "Role of the Champlain Canal," 642.

23. "In Hartford's Halls: Some Business of Interest before the Legislature," *The Day*, February 22, 1909, 1.

24. H. A. Surface, *The Lampreys of Central New York* (New York: National Fishery Congress Bulletin of the United States Fishery Commission, 1897), 212.

25. Quoted in John Richardson Dymond, John Limond Hart, and Andrew Lyle Pritchard, "The Fishes of the Canadian Waters of Lake Ontario," no. 37, *University of Toronto Studies: Publications of the Ontario Fisheries Research Laboratory* (Toronto: The University Library, 1929), 10.

26. Gage, *Lake and Brook Lampreys of New York*, 421–92.

27. Quoted in Dymond, Hart, and Pritchard, "Fishes of the Canadian Waters," 10.

28. Walter N. Koelz, *Fishing Industry of the Great Lakes*, Bureau of Fisheries Documents, no. 1001 (Washington, DC: Government Printing Office, 1926), 602.

29. John Richardson Dymond, "A Provisional List of the Fishes of Lake Erie," no. 4, *University of Toronto Studies: Publications of the Ontario Fisheries Research Laboratory* (Toronto: The University Library, 1922), 60.

30. Dymond, Hart, and Pritchard, "Fishes of the Canadian Waters," 11.

31. Alan Freeth Coventry, "Breeding Habits of the Land-Locked Sea Lamprey," no. 9, *University of Toronto Studies: Publications of the Ontario Fisheries Research Laboratory* (Toronto: The University Library, 1922): 131.

Chapter 2: The Deck of the *Beatrice M*

1. Carl L. Hubbs and T. E. B. Pope, "The Spread of the Sea Lamprey through the Great Lakes," *Transactions of the American Fisheries Society* 66, no. 1 (1937): 172–76.

2. Dymond, Hart, and Pritchard, "Fishes of the Canadian Waters," 11.

3. Coventry, "Breeding Habits of the Land-Locked Sea Lamprey," 129.

4. "Breaks Record in $10,000 Swim," *Spokesman Review*, August 24, 1929, 14.

5. "Lamprey Bites Girl, 'Gets Even' with Dad," *Battle Creek Enquirer*, August 21, 1953, 3.

6. Had it not been for Stuart helping me navigate, I would have never found Bluebird Landing or Mary Ann or Merle.

7. Alvera Pierson and Evelyn Lukkonen, "Focus: Bluebird Landing," *Duluth Township Landmarks*, December 1971.

8. Caitlyn Schuchhardt, "Taconite Mining in Silver Bay: A Tale of Extraction and Accumulation," *Arcadia*, no. 3 (2015), Rachel Carson Center for Environment and Society, http://www.environmentandsociety.org/arcadia/taco nite-mining-silver-bay-tale-extraction-and-accumulation

9. Vernon C. Applegate, "Natural History of the Sea Lamprey, *Petromyzon marinus*, in Michigan" (PhD diss., University of Michigan, 1950), 7.

10. "Sea Lamprey, Killer, Found in Lake Here," unidentified newspaper clipping dated May 29, 1936.

11. Hubbs and Pope, "Spread of the Sea Lamprey," 4.

12. Ibid., 5.

13. Typescript of the field notes of John Van Oosten and Fred A. Westerman, "Field Notes: Trip to Upper Michigan with Mr. Fred Westerman, November 21–December 3, 1937," John Van Oosten Library, US Geological Survey, Ann Arbor, Michigan, 9.

14. Ibid., 13.

15. See, for example, "Marine World Villain Preys on Great Lakes," *Reading Eagle*, March 13, 1938.

16. Typescript of annotated sea lamprey control meeting minutes by B. G. Herbert Johnson, "A History of Sea Lamprey Control in the Great Lakes," Great Lakes Fishery Commission Archives, Ann Arbor, Michigan, 3.

17. A subspecies of walleye often called "blue pike" (*Sander vitreus glaucus*) was fished to extinction in Lake Erie by the 1960s.

18. Typescript of minutes of the from the Great Lakes Sea Lamprey Committee meeting, 1947, Great Lakes Fishery Commission Archives, Ann Arbor, Michigan, 3.

Chapter 3: Nations Are Jolted to Action

1. The epigraph that opens this chapter is from a typescript of Henry O'Malley's opening remarks at the first conference of the Division of Scientific Inquiry, January 4–7, 1927, Great Lakes Fishery Commission Archives, Ann Arbor, Michigan, 561.

2. R. E. Coker, "Progress in Biological Inquiries: Report of the Division of Scientific Inquiry for the Fiscal Year 1920," Bureau of Fisheries Doc. 896 (Washington, DC: Government Printing Office), 7.

3. Clifton Johnson, *Highways and Byways of the Great Lakes* (New York: Macmillan, 1911), 126.

4. William B. Mershon, *The Passenger Pigeon* (New York: Outing Publishing, 1907).

5. Typescript of Walter Koelz's statement, "The Fisheries of the Great Lakes," at the first conference of the Division of Scientific Inquiry, January 4–7, 1927, Great Lakes Fishery Commission Archives, Ann Arbor, Michigan, 660.

6. Ibid., 661.

7. Margaret Beattie Bogue, *Fishing the Great Lakes: An Environmental History, 1783–1933* (Madison: University of Wisconsin Press, 2001), 278.

8. Typescript of meeting minutes, Walter Koelz speaking at the first meeting of the Division of Scientific Inquiry, Jan. 4–7, 1927, Great Lakes Fishery Commission Archives, Ann Arbor, Michigan, 662.

9. Reeve M. Bailey and Gerald R. Smith, "Origin and Geography of the Fish Fauna of the Laurentian Great Lakes Basin," *Canadian Journal of Fisheries and Aquatic Sciences* 38, no. 12 (1981): 1539–61.

10. Randy L. Eshenroder et al., *Ciscoes (Coregonus, subgenus Leucichthys) of the Laurentian Great Lakes and Lake Nipigon*, Great Lakes Fishery Commission Miscellaneous Publications, no. 2016–01 (Ann Arbor: Great Lakes Fishery Commission, 2016).

11. Typescript of John Van Oosten's speech at the third annual Great Lakes Fisheries Conference, Lansing, Michigan, December 5, 1928, Great Lakes Fishery Commission Archives, Ann Arbor, Michigan, 11.

12. Stuart Sivertson, conversation with the author, June 14, 2016.

13. Van Oosten and Westerman, "Field Notes," 8, 11, 14, 25, 34.

14. Typescript of John Van Oosten's speech "Fisheries Problems on Lakes Michigan and Superior," delivered at the Conference of Wisconsin Fishermen, Port Washington, Wisconsin, July 12, 1930, Great Lakes Fishery Commission Archives, Ann Arbor, Michigan, 5.

15. Typescript of Elmer Higgins's speech, "Waste: A Menace to the Fisheries," delivered at the Great Lakes Fishery Conference, Buffalo, New York, October 12, 1931, Great Lakes Fishery Commission Archives, Ann Arbor, Michigan, 2.

16. Typescript of John Van Oosten's speech, "Address Given before the Fisherman's Club of Chicago," March 30, 1935, Great Lakes Fishery Commission Archives, Ann Arbor, Michigan.

17. Ibid., 4.

18. Typescript of President Franklin D. Roosevelt's speech, "Speech of the President at the Dedication of the Thousand Islands Bridge," August 18, 1928, accessed March 13, 2019, http://www.fdrlibrary.marist.edu/_resources/images/msf/msf01204, 8.

19. Hubert R. Gallagher, A. G. Huntsman, D. J. Taylor, and John Van Oosten, "Report of the International Board of Inquiry for the Great Lakes Fisheries"

(1943), 1–24; American Association for the Advancement of Science, "Report of the International Board of Inquiry for the Great Lakes Fisheries." *Science* 99, no. 2558 (1944): 10.

20. Exchange of notes at Washington, DC, February 29, 1940, between Secretary of State Cordell Hull and Canadian Minister Loring Christie, "Board of Inquiry for Great Lakes Fisheries," Executive Agreement Series 182, https://www.loc.gov/law/help/us-treaties/bevans/b-ca-ust000006-0169.pdf

21. US Congress, House, Committee on Merchant Marine and Fisheries, *Commercial Fishing in the Great Lakes Area: Hearings before the Subcommittee on the Fisheries and Wildlife Conservation of the Committee on Merchant Marine and Fisheries*, 81st Cong., 1st sess., March 8–9, 1949, 2–5.

22. Dr. Marc Gaden, conversation with the author, October 16, 2018.

23. Great Lakes Fishery Commission, "Convention on Great Lakes Fisheries between the United States of America and Canada," accessed October 10, 2018, http://www.glfc.org/pubs/conv.htm

Chapter 4: First Stab at Sea Lamprey Control

1. David Shetter, *A Brief History of the Sea Lamprey Problem in Michigan Waters, Rep. No. 1086* (Ann Arbor: Institute for Fisheries Research, Division of Fisheries, Michigan Department of Conservation, in cooperation with the University of Michigan, 1947), 164.

2. David Shetter, *Results of the 1945 Operations at the Ocqueoc River Sea Lamprey Weir, Rep. No. 1015* (Ann Arbor: Institute for Fisheries Research, Division of Fisheries, Michigan Department of Conservation in cooperation with the University of Michigan, 1945), 1.

3. Jim Seelye, conversation with the author, September 26, 2015.

4. H. A. Surface, *The Lampreys of Central New York* (New York: National Fishery Congress Bulletin of the United States Fishery Commission, 1897), 213.

5. Quoted in Surface, *Lampreys of Central New York*, 214.

6. "Cornell University: Interesting Outcomes of Professor Gage's Study of the Lake Lamprey," *Boston Evening Transcript*, March 31, 1897, 10.

7. Surface, *Lampreys of Central New York*, 214.

8. Shetter, *Results of the 1945 Operations*, 3.

9. Typescript of John Van Oosten's personal notes, "Program for Control of Sea Lamprey on the Great Lakes Prepared by Dr. John Van Oosten, Fish and Wildlife Service," August 29, 1946, John Van Oosten Library, US Geological Survey, Ann Arbor, Michigan, 5.

10. US Congress, House, Committee on Merchant Marine and Fisheries, *Menace of the Sea Lamprey: Hearings before the Committee on Merchant Marine and Fisheries, House of Representatives on H.J. Res. 366 and H.J. Res. 367, Joint Resolutions Authorizing and Directing the Director of the Fish and Wildlife Service*

of the Department of the Interior to Investigate and Eradicate the Predatory Sea Lampreys of the Great Lakes, 79th Cong., 2nd sess., June 12–13, 1946, 15.

11. Van Oosten, *1946 Lamprey Meeting Notes*, 14.

12. Typescript of minutes of the Great Lakes Sea Lamprey Committee meeting, November 14–15, 1946, Great Lakes Fishery Commission Archives, Ann Arbor, Michigan, 1.

13. Ibid., 23.

14. Ibid., 18.

15. Ibid.

16. Johnny Mock, "Nets, Not Eels, Deplete Trout: Commercial Fishers Raise Familiar Cry," *Pittsburgh Press*, July 23, 1946.

17. Typescript of minutes of the Great Lakes Sea Lamprey Committee meeting, 1946, 17.

18. Applegate, "Natural History of the Sea Lamprey," 198.

19. Typescript of minutes of the Great Lakes Sea Lamprey Committee meeting, 1946, 11.

20. Vernon C. Applegate, "Observations on the Primeness of a Fall Collection of Muskrat" (MA thesis, University of Michigan, 1946).

21. Philip Wolf, "A Trap for the Capture of Fish and other Organisms Moving Downstream," *Transactions of the American Fisheries Society* 80, no. 1 (1951): 41–45.

22. Applegate, "Natural History of the Sea Lamprey."

23. Typescript of minutes of the Great Lakes Sea Lamprey Committee meeting, 1949, Great Lakes Fishery Commission Archives, Ann Arbor, Michigan, 1.

Chapter 5: Discovering a Chemical Assassin

1. Joseph B. Hunn, *Investigations in Fish Control: History of Acute Toxicity Tests with Fish, 1863–1987*, no. 98 (Washington DC: US Department of the Interior, Fish and Wildlife Service, 1989), 2.

2. Typescript of minutes of the Great Lakes Sea Lamprey Committee meeting, 1948, Great Lakes Fishery Commission Archives, Ann Arbor, Michigan, 4.

3. John Greenbank, "Selective Poisoning of Fish," *Transactions of the American Fisheries Society* 70, no. 1 (1941): 82.

4. Justin W. Leonard, "Notes on the Use of Derris as a Fish Poison," *Transactions of the American Fisheries Society* 68, no. 1 (1939): 269–80.

5. *Ammocoete* is a scientific term for larval sea lampreys.

6. Typescript of minutes of the Great Lakes Sea Lamprey Committee meeting, 1949, Great Lakes Fishery Commission Archives, Ann Arbor, Michigan, 31.

7. Jorge Fernandez-Cornejo, Craig Osteen, Richard Nehring, and Seth Wechsler, "Pesticide Use Peaked in 1981, Then Trended Downward, Driven by Technological Innovations and Other Factors," *USDA*, June 2, 2014, https://www.

ers.usda.gov/amber-waves/2014/june/pesticide-use-peaked-in-1981-then
-trended-downward-driven-by-technological-innovations-and-other-factors/

8. Typescript of minutes of the Great Lakes Sea Lamprey Committee meeting, 1950, Great Lakes Fishery Commission Archives, Ann Arbor, Michigan, 23.

9. Typescript of minutes of the Great Lakes Sea Lamprey Committee meeting, 1951, Great Lakes Fishery Commission Archives, Ann Arbor, Michigan, 63.

10. Rosalie Schnick, *Investigations in Fish Control: A Review of Literature on TFM (3-trifluoromethyl-4-nitrophenol) as a Lamprey Larvicide*, no. 44 (Washington DC, US Department of the Interior, Fish and Wildlife Service, Bureau of Sport Fisheries and Wildlife, 1972).

11. Typescript of the minutes of the Great Lakes Lake Trout and Sea Lamprey Committee meeting,1952, Great Lakes Fishery Commission Archives, Ann Arbor, Michigan, 50.

12. James W. Moffett, *Annual Report for Fiscal Year 1953: Great Lakes Fishery Investigations, Sea Lampreys* (Washington DC: US Department of the Interior, Fish and Wildlife Service, 1953). NOAA Central Library and the Climate Database Modernization Program, National Climate Data Center, 1.

13. Typescript of a letter from Vernon C. Applegate to Ralph Hile titled "Quarterly Report—Sea Lamprey Investigations—June to August, 1953," August 28, 1953, US Geological Survey, Hammond Bay Biological Station, Millersburg, Michigan.

14. Typescript of a letter from Vernon C. Applegate to James Moffett titled "Record Cards—Chemical Screening Tests," December 17, 1953, US Geological Survey, Hammond Bay Biological Station, Millersburg, Michigan.

15. Schnick, *Investigations in Fish Control*, 3.

16. Ibid., 4.

17. Ibid., 4–5.

18. Typescript of a letter from Vernon C. Applegate to James Moffett titled "Overtime Operations—Chemical Screening Tests," February 2, 1954, US Geological Survey, Hammond Bay Biological Station, Millersburg, Michigan.

19. Typescript of a letter from Vernon C. Applegate to Ralph Hile titled "Quarterly Report, December 1953–February 1954," February 26, 1954, US Geological Survey, Hammond Bay Biological Station, Millersburg, Michigan.

20. Tom Kuchenberg, *Reflections in a Tarnished Mirror: The Use and Abuse of the Great Lakes* (Sturgeon Bay, WI: Golden Glow, 1978), 64.

21. Vernon C. Applegate and Everett L. King Jr., "Comparative Toxicity of 3-Trifluormethyl-4-Nitrophenol (TFM) to Larval Lampreys and Eleven Species of Fishes," *Transactions of the American Fisheries Society* 91, no. 4 (1962): 342–45.

22. Vernon C. Applegate, John H. Howell, and Manning A Smith, "Use of Mononitrophenols containing Halogens as Selective Sea Lamprey Larvicides," *Science* 127, no. 3294 (1958): 336–38.

23. Ibid., 337.

24. Lloyd Lockhart, "Chemistry Tackles a Killer," *Star Weekly*, September 29, 1956.

25. Ibid.

26. *Vernon C. Applegate and John H. Howell v. Otto Scherer, Heinz Frensch, and Gerhard Stähler*, 332 F.2d 571 (C.C.P.A. 1964), accessed November 12, 2018, https://law.justia.com/cases/federal/appellate-courts/F2/332/571/327196/

27. Ibid.

28. Vernon C. Applegate et al., *Use of 3-Trifluormethyl-4-Nitrophenol as a Selective Sea Lamprey Larvicide*, no. 1 (Ann Arbor: Great Lakes Fishery Commission, 1961).

29. "All Eels Die in Test River," *Milwaukee Journal*, May 17, 1958, 4.

Chapter 6: Multinational AIS Control

1. Typescript of the Great Lakes Fishery Commission annual report for the year 1962, Great Lakes Fishery Commission Archives, Ann Arbor, Michigan, 9.

2. Rudolf Gönnert, "Results of Laboratory and Field Trials with the Molluscicide Bayer 73," *Bulletin of the World Health Organization* 25 (1961): 483.

3. Dorance C. Brege et al., "Factors Responsible for the Reduction in Quantity of the Lampricide, TFM, Applied Annually in Streams Tributary to the Great Lakes from 1979 to 1999," *Journal of Great Lakes Research* 29 (2003): 500–509.

4. US Environmental Protection Agency, "Reregistration Eligibility Decision (RED) 3-Trifluoro-Methyl-4-Nitro-Phenol and Niclosamide," EPA 738-R-99-007, November 1999, https://nepis.epa.gov/Exe/ZyPDF.cgi/901A0600.PDF?Dockey=901A0600.PDF

5. Michael A. Boogaard, Terry D. Bills, and David A. Johnson, "Acute Toxicity of TFM and a TFM/Niclosamide Mixture to Selected Species of Fish, Including Lake Sturgeon (*Acipenser Fulvescens*) and Mudpuppies (*Necturus Maculosus*), in Laboratory and Field Exposures," *Journal of Great Lakes Research* 29 (2003): 529–41.

6. Ellen Marsden et al., "Sea Lamprey Control in Lake Champlain," *Journal of Great Lakes Research* 29 (2003): 655–76.

7. John H. Carey and Michael E. Fox, "Photodegradation of the Lampricide 3-Trifluoromethyl-4-Nitrophenol (TFM): 1. Pathway of the Direct Photolysis in Solution," *Journal of Great Lakes Research* 7, no. 3 (1981): 234–41.

8. Verdel K. Dawson, "Environmental Fate and Effects of the Lampricide Bayluscide: A Review," *Journal of Great Lakes Research* 29 (2003): 475–92.

9. Lee H. Hanson, "Sterilization of Sea Lampreys (*Petromyzon marinus*) by Immersion in an Aqueous Solution of Bisazir," *Canadian Journal of Fisheries and Aquatic Sciences* 38, no. 10 (1981): 1285–89.

10. Larry P. Schleen et al., "Development and Implementation of an Integrated

Program for Control of Sea Lampreys in the St. Marys River," *Journal of Great Lakes Research* 29 (2003): 677–93.

11. Ronald J. Scholefield and James G. Seelye, *Resistance to 3-trifluoromethyl-4-nitrophenol (TFM) in Sea Lamprey*, no. 56 (Ann Arbor, MI: Great Lakes Fishery Commission, 1990).

12. Erin S. Dunlop et al., "Rapid Evolution Meets Invasive Species Control: The Potential for Pesticide Resistance in Sea Lamprey," *Canadian Journal of Fisheries and Aquatic Sciences* 75, no. 1 (2017): 152–68.

13. Typescript of minutes of the Great Lakes Sea Lamprey Committee meeting, 1949, Great Lakes Fishery Commission Archives, Ann Arbor, Michigan, 34.

14. See information about the Fish Pass Project at the Great Lakes Fishery Commission website, http://www.glfc.org/fishpass.php (accessed November 15, 2018).

15. Jason D. Bals and C. Michael Wagner, "Behavioral Responses of Sea Lamprey (*Petromyzon marinus*) to a Putative Alarm Cue Derived from Conspecific and Heterospecific Sources," *Behaviour* 149, no. 9 (2012): 901–23.

16. Jeramiah J. Smith et al., "Sequencing of the Sea Lamprey (*Petromyzon marinus*) Genome Provides Insights into Vertebrate Evolution," *Nature Genetics* 45, no. 4 (2013): 415.

Conclusion

1. Johnson, "History of Sea Lamprey Control," 46.

2. Tribal members of the Upper Great Lakes region have fished these fresh waters since time beyond record. Members signed several treaties with the US government in the mid-1800s, treaties which ceded tribal lands yet maintained tribal members' rights to fish and hunt those lands. The treaties were subsequently ignored when territories became states, and states began to regulate natural resources. Tribal members were arrested and prosecuted for exercising their right to fish during the mid-1900s. Fewer tribal members fished during this period, which was around the same time sea lampreys began devastating the fishery. But members fought back for their rights. The *Gurnoe* decision, January 26, 1972, ruled in favor of the Bad River and Red Cliff tribes' fishing rights in Lake Superior (see https://law.justia.com/cases/wisconsin/supreme-court/1972/state-92-4-1.html; see also http://www.glifwc.org/publications/index.html; accessed November 15, 2018). The *Voigt* decision, January 25, 1983, affirmed treaty rights of Lake Superior Ojibwe. Hunting, fishing and gathering rights for tribal members were again reserved and protected (see https://sites.google.com/site/lcooccact31/home/t, accessed November 15, 2018).

3. Marc Gaden interviewed Bill Mattes on this day while I made notes.

4. For more information, see the Great Lakes Restoration Initiative website, accessed November 15, 2018, https://www.glri.us/

INDEX

AIS (aquatic invasive species)
  adaptability of, 30, 33
  defined, 22–23
  in Great Lakes ecosystem, 18, 33
  human-related vectors for, 23–24,
    26
  native fish affected by, 24, 25, 32–
    33, 153
  resources for controlling, 23
alarm cues, 143
alewife (*Alosa pseudoharengus*), 67,
  118
alien species (term), 23
Allen, Don, 85
Alosa pseudoharengus (alewife), 67,
  118
Ameiurus nebulosus (bullhead), 37,
  38
American brook lamprey (*Lethen-
    teron appendix*), 14–15
American eels, 34–35
American Fisheries Society, 70
*American Highways and Byways of
    the Great Lakes* (Johnson), 60
anadromy, 13–14, 33–34
anatomy and physiology of sea lampreys
  anadromy, 13–14, 33–34
  migratory changes in, 7–8
  overview, 4–5, 15
  pheromones, 8–9, 13, 16, 142–43

reproduction, 8–10
sensory features, 6, 159n4
transition to parasitic stage, 12–13,
  16
Anderson, H. E., 56
Anderson, William "Bill," 127–28
Applegate, Vernon
  biochemical assays supervised
    by, 106, 110–11, 113–14, 115, 116,
    118–19
  carp problem recognized by, 120
  on chemical immunity, 122
  chemical research questions, 117
  Dowlap testing, 118
  electric weir research, 111, 112, 113,
    121
  Hammond Bay Biological Station
    directed by, 104
  "inclined screen trap," 101
  on multimethod control approach,
    141
  on necessity of sea lamprey control,
    120–21
  patent applications, 118, 121, 125–26
  sea lamprey palatability studied by,
    96–97
  sea lamprey research, 3, 8, 12, 98,
    99–101
  TFM testing, 120, 126–29
"Asian carp," 30–31, 32, 148
Atlantic salmon (*Salmo salar*), 34

Bad River, Wisconsin, 151
Bailey, Reeve, 63
ballast water, 24–25, 26–27
Balling, L. C., 126–27
Bartell, Dave, 136
Basel, Alfred, 47
Bayer 73 (Baylucide), 132, 137, 140–41
Bay Port Fish Company, 154
Beatrice M, 45, 48, 53
Bell Brother's Fishery, 48
Berlinski Creek, Michigan, 134
bighead carp (*Hypopthalmichthys nobilis*), 30, 31–32
Black, Frank, 79
black carp (*Mylopharyngodon piceus*), 30
Blackhurst, A. O., 74
Black Mallard River, Michigan, 124–25
Blind River, Ontario, 152–53
Bluebird Landing, 47–51
Bowers, Hans, 92
Bradley, Frederick Van Ness, 87
Braem, Bob, 89, 92
Brule River, Wisconsin, 112
bullhead (*Ameiurus nebulosus*), 37, 38
burbot (*Lota lota*), 6, 93, 94, 130
burrowing, 10–12

Canada, sea lamprey control efforts in, 71–72, 76, 83, 95, 131, 133, 135, 149
carp
 "Asian," 30–31, 32, 148
 bighead, 30, 31–32
 black, 30
 common, 23
 grass, 30, 31
 silver, 30, 31–32
Carp Creek (Black Mallard River), Michigan, 124–25
Cayuga Lake, New York, 37–38, 78
Chambers, Charlie, 136

chemical controls. *See* Dowlap; lampricides; TFM
chestnut lampreys (*Ichthyomyzon castaneus*), 14, 15
Chinook salmon, 145
Chippewa Ottawa Resource Authority (CORA), 152
Christie, Loring, 71
cisco. *See* native deepwater cisco; shortjaw cisco
Cladophora algae, 28
Clostridium botulinum, 28, 29–30
"coho fever," 19, 149
coho (Pacific) salmon, 19–20, 145, 146–47, 148, 149
commercial fishing industry, Great Lakes
 advancements in, 67
 annual yields, 1–3, 19, 22, 61–62, 65
 Canadian fisheries, 95
 early sea lamprey control efforts, 44–47, 56–57
 formal sea lamprey control efforts and, 59, 70–75, 92, 95
 gill net issues, 43, 67, 68
 international cooperation in, 69–76, 95
 invasive mussels and, 152, 153, 154
 on Lake Ontario, 39
 mining pollution and, 51
 overfishing and, 51–52, 56, 62, 93
 regulation of, 59, 62–63, 64–75
 sea lamprey and saleable harvests, 1–3, 56, 94, 95, 152
 smelt and, 19, 20–21, 22
 tribal and First Nations fisheries, 151–52
 waste in, 67–68
common carp, 23
Convention on Great Lakes Fisheries, 72, 74, 76

Cooper, Gerald, 98–99
copper sulfate, 91, 108, 109
CORA (Chippewa Ottawa Resource
    Authority), 152
Coregonus clupeaformis. See lake
    whitefish
Coregonus spp. See native deepwater
    cisco
Coregonus zenithicus (shortjaw cisco),
    67
Coventry, A. F., 41, 43, 88
Crewe, Alexander, 40
Ctenopharyngodon idella (grass
    carp), 30, 31
Cuddy, Doug, 144

Day, Albert, 72
Deason, Hilary, 64, 77, 86–87
DeMille, Matt, 147
Department of Fisheries and Oceans
    Canada, 76, 149
Department of Fisheries and Oceans
    Sea Lamprey Control Centre
    (SLCC), 133, 135
Diporeia, 27–28
Division of Scientific Inquiry, 59,
    61–62
Domke, Ben, 125
Dowlap
    field testing of, 118, 120, 121, 123,
        125, 128
    in Lamprecid formula, 131
    vs. TFM, 120, 127
Dreissena polymorpha (zebra mussel),
    24–26
Dreissena rostriformis bugensis
    (quagga mussel), 24–26
dreissenid mussels
    commercial fishing impact, 152,
        153, 154
    ecological impact of, 26, 27–28,
        29–30

human-related vectors for, 24–26
    quagga mussels, 24–26
    reproduction of, 28
    round gobies and, 29–30
    zebra mussels, 24–26
Dubin, Don, 149–50
Dymond, John, 40, 41, 74, 88

Ebel, Wes, 92
Ectopistes migratorius (passenger
    pigeons), 60–61
electrofishing, 84–89, 142
Elliot Creek, Michigan, 123, 124, 128
Environmental Protection Agency
    (EPA), 137
Erie Canal, 34, 36, 39
Eshenroder, Randy, 34, 36

feeding habits of sea lampreys, 5, 10,
    12, 13, 14
Ferguson, Homer, 87
Finger Lakes, New York, 35, 37–38,
    76
First Nations fisheries, 151–52, 169n2
fisheries. See commercial fishing
    industry
Flory, William, 86
Frank, Robert, 101
Frensch, Heinz, 125
Fulmar, 63, 68

Gaden, Marc, 74–75
Gage, Simon, 36, 37, 38, 78–79
Gallagher, Hubert, 72
gender, in sea lamprey control crews,
    138–39
gill nets, 67, 68
GLIFWC (Great Lakes Indian Fish
    and Wildlife Commission),
    151–52
GLSLC (Great Lakes Sea Lamprey
    Committee), 89–95

goby, round (*Neogobius melanostomus*), 29–30
Gordon, Seth, 70
Gorenflo, Tony, 152
grass carp (*Ctenopharyngodon idella*), 30, 31
Great Depression, 42, 65, 68, 77
Great Lakes Basin
  glaciation and formation of, 35–36
  sea lamprey invasion throughout, 42, 53–54, 56–58
Great Lakes ecosystem
  appreciation for, 155–56
  as connected system, 39–40
  introduced species, 19–20, 23, 145, 146–47, 148
  invasive species, 18, 33
  native species, 14, 15, 28 (*see also* lake trout; lake whitefish)
  predictability of, 32–33
Great Lakes Fisheries Act (1956), 149
Great Lakes Fisheries Conference, 64–65
Great Lakes Fishery Commission, 76, 131, 133, 149
Great Lakes Indian Fish and Wildlife Commission (GLIFWC), 151–52
Great Lakes Sea Lamprey Committee (GLSLC), 89–95
Great Lakes Water Quality Agreement, 139
Greenbank, John, 108
Greene, Bill, 85–86
Grinold, Denny, 147–48

habitat and range of sea lampreys, 11–12, 13–14, 33–36, 139
halogenated nitrosalicylanilides, 132
Hammond Bay Biological Station (HBBS)
  acquisition of, 103

electric weir development at, 105, 112, 113
  facilities, 104
  funding issues, 113
  lampricides studied at, 105–7, 109–11, 113–24, 125, 126–27, 132
  records of biochemical assays, 114–15, 119
  sterilization techniques developed at, 140
Hazzard, Albert, 106
Health Canada Pest Management Regulatory Agency, 137
Heinrich, John, 144, 145
Henry I, King, 96
Herbst, Seth, 31
Hibbard's Creek, Wisconsin, 83
Higgins, Elmer, 67–68
Hile, Ralph, 113, 116
H. J. Res. 366 (1946), 87–88
Hoff, Mike, 32
hosts for sea lampreys
  characteristics of, 5–6, 14
  survival of, 5, 14
  wounds on, 2, 6, 7, 38, 94, 95, 145, 152
Howell, John, 118, 121, 125, 127–28
Hubbs, Carl, 54
Hull, Cordell, 71
Huntsman, A. G., 72
Hypopthalmichthys molitrix (silver carp), 30, 31–32
Hypopthalmichthys nobilis (bighead carp), 30, 31–32

Ichthyomyzon castaneus (chestnut lampreys), 14, 15
Ichthyomyzon fossor (northern brook lamprey), 14, 15
Ichthyomyzon unicuspis (silver lampreys), 14, 15

integrated pest management (IPM),
141–42
International Board of Inquiry, 72
"introduced" vs. "invasive," 22–23
introduction of species, defined, 23
Invading Species Awareness Program,
Ontario, 23
invasive species. See AIS (aquatic
invasive species)
IPM (integrated pest management),
141–42

Johnson, Clifton, 60
Juilleret, Earl, 44
Juilleret, Edith, 44

Kalamazoo River, Michigan, 136
Kaministiquia River, Ontario, 136
Katzenbach, Nicholas, 17
Koelz, Walter, 59–60, 61–64, 65
Kolbe, Carl, 95
Koon, Ellie, 138–39
Kortman, Cliff
HBBS property management,
103–6
introduction to sea lamprey
research, 1–3, 102
lampricides studied by, 106, 107,
118, 119–20, 122, 123, 124, 125, 127
life cycle illustration, 105
Kutchenberg, Tom, 116

Lagler, Karl, 99
LaHaie, Steve, 150–51
Lake Erie
connection to other Great Lakes,
39, 40
early sea lamprey sightings in, 40,
42, 56–57
Lake Huron
connection to other Great Lakes,
39–40

early sea lamprey sightings in, 53
newer AIS in, 154
sea lamprey impact on, 1–3, 53, 56,
83
St. Marys River efforts and, 139
Lake Michigan
connection to other Great Lakes,
39–40
early sea lamprey sightings in, 42
sea lamprey impact on, 1–3, 56
Lake Ontario
connection to other Great Lakes,
39, 40
habitat degradation, 39
lampricide treatments, 144–45
as native vs. nonnative sea lamprey
range, 34–36
salmon stocking, 146–47
sea lamprey impact on, 37–38
sea lamprey population growth in,
40–41
sea lamprey routes into, 39
sport-fishing industry, 147
Lake Superior
connection to other Great Lakes,
40, 55
sea lampreys found in, 55–56, 113
TFM field testing and, 127
lake trout (Salvelinus namaycush)
commercial yields of, 1–3, 45, 47,
62, 65
gill nets and, 67, 68
population decline, 1–3, 53, 83, 93, 95
rainbow smelt and, 20–21, 67
scarring and saleability of, 2, 94, 95
as sea lamprey host, 5–6
lake whitefish (Coregonus clupeaformis)
commercial yields of, 46, 62, 65, 83
dreissenid mussel impact on, 28,
153
population crash, 62

Lamprecid 2770, 121, 129, 131
lampreys, native, 14, 15
lampricides. *See also* Dowlap; TFM
  annual monitoring, 135, 137–38
  annual treatments, 133–34, 135–38
  application cutbacks, 152
  degradation of, 138
  field testing of, 118, 120, 121, 123,
    125, 127–29, 132
  lab testing of, 105–7, 109–11, 113–
    24, 125, 126–27, 132
  Lamprecid 2770, 121, 129, 131
  mononitrophenols, 114, 116–17, 118,
    119–20, 121
  nontarget mortality, 135, 137–38
  pesticide movement (1950s), 108–9
  resistance/immunity to, 122, 140
  risks of, 91, 106
  rotenone, 106, 108, 109
  selectivity of, 108–9, 113, 118, 135,
    138
LaPan, Steve, 146
larval stage, 6–7, 10–12, 101, 123,
  166n5
Lennon, Robert, 114
Leopold, Aldo, 60–61
Lethenteron appendix (American
  brook lamprey), 14–15
Little Billie's Creek (Elliot Creek),
  Michigan, 123, 124, 128
Little River, Wisconsin, 92
Little Thessalon River, Ontario, 83–84
Lockhart, Lloyd, 120–21, 122
Lota lota (burbot), 6, 93, 94, 130
Ludington, Michigan, Fish and Wild-
  life Service station, 133
Lukkonen, Evelyn Sandberg, 47–49,
  51
Lukkonen, Tim, 47–49

MacDonald, Jim, 20–21
MacKay, Hector, 65, 88

Mackenzie King, William, 71, 72
Magnetawan River, Ontario, 134
Makauskas, Ed, 148–49
Marquette, Michigan, 56, 113, 133
mating, 8–10, 13
Mattes, Bill, 151–52
McDonald, D. M., 65
McKernan, D. L., 74
media coverage of sea lampreys, 16–
  17, 51, 54, 56
Mertz, Beatrice, 44–46, 47, 48
Mertz, Clarence, 53
Mertz, Katherine, 44–46, 48
Mertz, Louis, 44, 45
Mertz, Mary, 44
Mertz Fishery, 47, 53
Meyer, Fred, 137
Michigan Department of Conserva-
  tion, 88
Michigan Department of Natural
  Resources (MDNR), 19
Michigan Fish Commission, 3, 18
migration, 6–8, 13
Miller, Mike, 146–47
mining industry, ecological impact
  of, 51
Mississippi River, 39
Mock, Johnny, 93
Moffett, James
  as GLSLC director, 101–2, 108
  lampricide field tests, 128, 129, 132
  lampricide lab research, 105, 108–9,
    112–13, 115
mononitrophenols, 114, 116–17, 118,
  119–20, 121. *See also* TFM
Morone saxatilis (striped bass), 14
Mosquito River, Michigan, 127–29
Moyle, Clarence, 118
Muntinga, W. H., 64, 68
mussels, native, 28
mussels, quagga, 24–26. *See also*
  dreissenid mussels

mussels, zebra, 24–26. *See also* dreis-
    senid mussels
Mylopharyngodon piceus (black carp),
    30

Nalepa, Tom, 27–28
NANPCA (Nonindigenous Aquatic
    Nuisance and Control Act,
    1990), 26
Nash, C. W., 37–38
National Invasive Species Act (NISA,
    1996), 27
native deepwater cisco (*Coregonus spp.*)
    as animal feed, 66, 67
    commercial harvest and processing
        of, 61–62, 66, 67, 69
    extinct and threatened species, 60,
        63, 67
    Koelz's study of, 63
    population crash, 62
    sea lampreys as threat to, 60, 61
native lamprey species, Great Lakes,
    14, 15
native mussel species, Great Lakes, 28
Nelson, Cyril, 79, 81
Neogobius melanostomus (round
    goby), 29–30
nest building, 8
New York Department of Environ-
    mental Conservation (NYDEC),
    144–45, 146
Niagara Falls, 39, 40
NISA (National Invasive Species Act,
    1996), 27
Nonindigenous Aquatic Nuisance
    and Control Act (NANPCA,
    1990), 26
Norelius, Martha, 44
Norgren, Merle, 47, 49, 51
northern brook lamprey (*Ichthyomy-
    zon fossor*), 14, 15
Norton, Marvin, 53, 77

NYDEC (New York Department of
    Environmental Conservation),
    144–45, 146
Nyman, Bryan, 152–53
Nyman, Leonard, 152–53

Ocqueoc River, Michigan
    CCC camp, 1, 99, 102
    lampricide treatment, 141
    mechanical weir and trap, 78–84
    sea lamprey control proposal, 77
    sea lampreys sighted and studied
        in, 8, 51–53, 145, 156
    volunteer control efforts in, 77–78
O'Malley, Henry, 59
Ontario Department of Lands and
    Forests (ODLF), 95
Ontario Ministry of Natural
    Resources (OMNR), 95, 146
Osmerus mordax. See rainbow smelt
osmoregulation, 33, 34
overfishing, commercial, 51–52, 56,
    62, 93

Pacific salmon, 19–20, 145, 146–47,
    148, 149
Paczocha, Frank, 54
Pancake River, Ontario, 131
parasitic stage, 12–13, 16, 34
passenger pigeons (*Ectopistes migra-
    torius*), 60–61
Patterson, Matt, 94
Peterson, Emmet, 85
pheromones, 8–9, 13, 16, 142–43
Pierson, Alvera, 51
Plath, Emil, 96
pollution, 51, 96, 139
Pope, T. E. B., 54
predators of sea lampreys, 14
Presque Isle County Sportsman's
    Club, 77
Pritchard, A. L., 74

producers (infested streams), 131
Purvis, George, 83
Purvis Brothers Fishery, 83, 84

quagga mussel (*Dreissena rostriformis bugensis*), 24–26. *See also* dreissenid mussels

rainbow smelt (*Osmerus mordax*)
    commercial fishing and, 19, 21, 22
    ecological impact of, 20–21, 67
    introduction of, 18–19, 23
    population growth, 19, 118
    recreational harvest of, 19–20, 21, 22
Rivers, Cecil, 140
Robertson, John, 148
Roosevelt, Franklin D., 71, 72
rotenone, 106, 108, 109
round goby (*Neogobius melanostomus*), 29–30
Rude, Mark, 21–22

salmon, Atlantic (*Salmo salar*), 34
salmon, Chinook, 145
salmon, Pacific. *See* Pacific salmon
Salmo salar (Atlantic salmon), 34
Salvelinus namaycush. See lake trout
Sault Ste. Marie, Ontario, 21, 133
Sawyer, Philip, 109–10, 114, 116
Scherer, Otto, 125–26
Schleen, Larry, 139–40
Schneberger, Edward, 88
Schnick, Rosalie "Roz," 114, 137
sea lamprey (*Petromyzon marinus*)
    anatomy and physiology of (*see* anatomy and physiology)
    commercial harvest impacted by, 1–3, 56, 62, 65, 94, 95, 152
    as culinary delicacy, 36
    early sightings of, 8, 40, 42, 51–54, 56–57
    ecological impact of, 1–3, 37–38, 83

feeding behavior, 5–6, 10, 12, 13, 14
    Great Lakes Basin invaded by, 42, 53–54, 56–58
    habitat and range of (*see* habitat and range of sea lampreys)
    hitchhiking abilities of, 43
    host scarring from, 2, 6, 7, 38, 94, 95, 145, 152
    larval stage, 6–7, 10–12, 101, 123, 166n5
    life cycle of, 6–7, 13, 14, 105
    as living fossils, 16
    mating behavior, 8–10, 13
    media images of, 16–17
    migration of, 6–8
    names for, 8, 35, 37
    native functions of, 14
    nesting behavior, 8
    palatability of, 95–97
    parasitic stage, 12–13, 16, 34
    predators of, 14
    research uses for, 16
    sport fishing impacted by, 47–51, 147, 148, 149, 152
    threatened status of, 14, 36–37
    toxins accumulated in, 95–96
sea lamprey control
    chemical (*see* lampricides)
    cost of, 76
    crews, 138–39
    education and outreach, 147–48
    electric weirs, 111, 112, 113, 121, 142
    electrofishing, 84–89, 142
    vs. eradication, 97–99
    evolution of, 133–39
    funding for, 79, 88, 102, 113, 140
    genetic tools, 143
    international regulations and, 70–74, 75–76, 131, 133, 149
    legislative efforts, 86–87
    mechanical weirs (*see* weirs, mechanical)

multi-tool approach to, 141–43
in New York, 76, 78–79, 80
on Ocqueoc River (see Ocqueoc
River)
pheromones, 143
recreational fishing community
attitudes about, 146–50
in St. Marys River, 139–40
success and ongoing necessity of,
131, 144, 145–48, 149, 152, 154
tribal and First Nations attitudes
about, 151–52, 169n2
Seelye, Jim, 77–78
semelparity, defined, 14
Shetter, David, 57–58, 81
shortjaw cisco (C. zenithicus), 67
silver carp (Hypopthalmichthys molitrix), 30, 31–32
silver lampreys (Ichthyomyzon unicuspis), 14, 15
Simonis, Floyd, 101
Sironen, Mary Ann, 47–51
Sivertson, Stuart, 47, 51
Skaggs, Beatrice (née Mertz), 44–46,
47
SLCC (Department of Fisheries and
Oceans Sea Lamprey Control
Centre), 133, 135
Smeltanias, 20, 21
"smelt fever," 19–20. See also rainbow
smelt (Osmerus mordax)
Smith, Gerald, 63
Smith, Oliver, 92–93
Smith Bros. Fisheries, 92–93
Soulier, Ervin, 151
sport-fishing industry, 47–51, 147, 148,
149, 152
Stähler, Gerhard, 125
St. Lawrence River, Ontario, 40
St. Lawrence Seaway Management
Corporation, 27, 71
St. Marys River, 40, 55, 139–40

Stop Aquatic Hitchhikers Program,
USFWS, 23
striped bass (Morone saxatilis), 14
Sturgeon River, Ontario, 82
Sullivan, Leo, 133, 134
Sullivan, Tim, 133, 135–37
Surface, H. A., 37, 38, 78, 79, 80
swimmers, sea lampreys and, 43–44
Swink, Bill, 78
swordfish (Xiphias gladius), 14

Tack, Peter, 95
Tanner, Howard, 19–20
Taylor, D. J., 72
TFM (3-trifluoromethyl-4-nitrophe-
nol)
annual treatment protocol, 133–
37
Bayer 73 added to, 132
environmental screening of, 137
field testing of, 127–29, 132
lab testing of, 118, 119–20, 121,
125–27
as Lamprecid 2770, 121, 129, 131
multinational use of, 131
resistance to, 140–41
Thompson, Robbie, 82
Thousand Islands Bridge, 71
Todd, Andy, 146
Tody, Wayne, 19–20
Torch Lake, Michigan, 18–19
traps, 78, 79, 80, 83, 90–91, 101, 142
tribal fisheries, 151–52, 169n2
Truman, Harry, 87–88

US Bureau of Fisheries, 59, 63
US Fish and Wildlife Service
(USFWS)
AIS control resources, 23
creation of, 72–73
Great Lakes Fishery Commission
and, 76

US Fish and Wildlife Service (USFWS) (*continued*)
Hammond Bay Fishery Laboratory acquired by, 103
Michigan Department of Conservation and, 88
Michigan stations, 133
National Fishery Research lab, 137
USGS Great Lakes Science Center, 76, 103–4
USS Lamprey (SS-372), 17

Van Oosten, John
on control *vs.* eradication, 97–98
early sightings confirmed by, 42, 154
humor used by, 69
on International Board of Inquiry, 72
international/national cooperation promoted by, 69–70, 88–99, 101
legislative hearing statement, 86, 87
"national fish policy" advocated by, 70
nontarget net mortality identified by, 67, 68
Ocqueoc control experiment, 77
population statistics advocated by, 65
sea lamprey invasion studied by, 53, 54–56, 64, 77
sea lamprey palatability studied by, 97
Ver Duin, Claude, 74, 86, 93, 131
Voigt, Lester, 74

Walsh, Vivian Lee, 43–44
water quality, 28, 139
Weichel, Alvin, 72–73, 75, 87
weirs, electric, 111, 112, 113, 121, 142
weirs, low-head, 142
weirs, mechanical
in Finger Lakes, 76, 78–79, 80
improvements to, 90
in integrated pest management, 142
in Ocqueoc River, 78–84
traps used with, 78, 79, 80, 83, 90–91, 101
Welland Canal, 39, 40
West Davignon River, Ontario, 131
Westerman, Fred
lake trout losses to gill nets, 67
"national fish policy" advocated by, 70
sea lamprey invasion studied by, 54–56, 64, 65, 88, 154
Weymouth, Bob, 134
Wilcox, Ralph, 127, 129–30
Wilder, Burt, 36, 37, 78–79
Williams, Tod, 154
Wolf, Philip, 101
World War I, 42, 62
World War II, 1, 42, 57, 78
Write, Stillman, 108

Xiphias gladius (swordfish), 14

zebra mussel (*Dreissena polymorpha*), 24–26. *See also* dreissenid mussels